I *Am* Reading

KATHY COLLINS • MATT GLOVER

I Am Reading

Nurturing Young Children's
**Meaning Making and
Joyful Engagement**
with Any Book

HEINEMANN
Portsmouth, NH

Heinemann
361 Hanover Street
Portsmouth, NH 03801–3912
www.heinemann.com

Offices and agents throughout the world

The authors and publisher wish to thank those who have generously given permission to reprint borrowed material:

Cover and excerpts from *Knuffle Bunny: A Cautionary Tale*. Copyright © 2004 by Mo Willems. Originally published by Hyperion Books for Children. Used with permission.

Cover and excerpts from *Three Billy Goats Gruff*. Copyright © 1998 by Stephen Carpenter. Used by permission of HarperCollins Publishers.

Excerpts from *Go, Dog. Go!* by P. D. Eastman. Copyright © 1961 by P. D. Eastman. Copyright renewed 1989 by Mary L. Eastman. Used by permission of Random House Children's Books, a division of Random House LLC. All rights reserved.

Excerpts from *The Very Hungry Caterpillar* by Eric Carle. Copyright ©1969 & 1987 by Eric Carle. Used with permission by the Eric Carle Studio.

Excerpts from *Clip-Clop*. Copyright © 2006 Nicola Smee. World rights Boxer Books Limited. All rights reserved. Boxer® is a Registered Trademark of Boxer Books Limited.

Credits continue on page vi.

Cataloging-in-Publication Data is on file with the Library of Congress.
ISBN: 978-0-325-05092-8

Editor: Zoë Ryder White
Production Editor: Sonja S. Chapman
Cover and interior design: Suzanne Heiser
Typesetter: Kim Arney
Manufacturing: Steve Bernier

Printed in the United States of America on acid-free paper

19   18   17   16   15   PAH   1   2   3   4   5

Dedicated to

RENÉE DINNERSTEIN

A great friend

whose advocacy for young children

and their teachers

is a constant inspiration

CONTENTS

VIDEO CONTENTS

*Bookmark
https://heinemann.com
/IAmReading to easily
access a menu of the
video clips.*

ACKNOWLEDGMENTS

Goodness, where do we start? This book may have our names listed as coauthors on the cover, but we consider this book to be a crowd-sourced endeavor. We've received support and inspiration from so many people who are teaching and raising children all over the world.

We begin by thanking all of our friends who have shared videos and stories of their young children reading. Maggie Moon, Erin Kent, Laurie Smilak, Carol Ryan, Erica Radford, Dawn Brennan, and Zoë Ryder White, you gave us both the teacher and the parent perspectives, reminding us that the best teaching arises from a place of love and respect for children.

We want to thank the many educators who welcomed us, and our video equipment, into their schools to observe their children. The open doors at Panda Path and Lion Lane in Houston, Bangkok International School, Concordia School in Shanghai, The American School of Dohu, the Mason, Centerville, and Madeira schools in Ohio, Lawrence Township in Indiana, and Blue Springs in Missouri, opened up so many lines of thinking that took shape in this book. We thank the New Franklin School in Portsmouth, New Hampshire, for welcoming us into their kindergarten world.

We want to thank the teachers who let us watch them teach and gave us time to learn from their children. This book would not have been possible without the professional generosity of Sharee Cantrell, Sara Hannes, Patty Horan, Tammy Westrick, Amy Horstman, Mary-Ann MacPherson, Barb Pearson, Ann Ellis, Lisa Hilliker, Bridget Glover, Maggie LaBoube, Megan Hood, Jen Phillips, Karen Davidson, Joann Abreau, Amy Cowgill, Molly Dahl, Megan Ralston, Soroya Smith, Krissy Hufnagel, Jenny Davis, Christie Motz, Michelle Hastings, Robyn Thomas, Katrina Theilmann, and Lyn Hennigar.

Mary Alice Berry gave us the gift of her time, teaching, and insightful thinking as she made videos and shared her classroom work with us. We are grateful.

We want to thank Renée Dinnerstein and Katie Ray for all the ways they've guided our thinking about the wonders of early childhood.

We owe a bottomless debt of gratitude to the work of so many early childhood literacy educators, especially Marie Clay, Elizabeth Sulzby, Brian Cambourne, and Vivian Gussin Paley. Their field-changing research about young children and early literacy has informed so much of our thinking.

We are grateful to the team at Heinemann for taking good care of a book that means so much to us. It wouldn't have been possible without Sherry Day and Roberta Lew, who figured out the permissions and video aspects of this project. We had no idea what an undertaking that would be! We appreciate the tireless efforts of Sonja Chapman, Anthony Marvullo, Eric Chalek, Michael Grover, and Cindy Black for all of the ways they guided us on the path from draft manuscript to publication.

We are enormously grateful to Zoë Ryder White, our editor who was actually more like a coauthor. She enabled us to realize our vision for this book because she shared it, too. Early on, Zoë sent us a photo of her young daughter Anna sitting on the toilet in cowboy boots and a tutu reading a fat book of fairy tales. This photo served as our lodestar, representing perfectly the balance of reading work and play and an appreciation for the eccentricities of childhood that we hope are conveyed on every page.

We want to acknowledge our writing partnership because the process of working on this together for the last couple of years has been a pleasure and, dare we say, *fun*? Fortunately, our ideas and our procrastination habits are synchronized. Now that we've finished this project, we can get back to the important work of arguing over our baseball teams and finding the next great binge-worthy television series to recommend to each other.

We are so grateful to our families for their unwavering support. Kathy would like to thank her husband, Ian, and their children, Owen and Theo, for everything they are and all they do to make life sweet. She'd also like to thank her mom for modeling a life full of meaningful work.

Matt would like to thank his wife and amazing teacher, Bridget. Much of the early research for this book was done in the preschool special education class where she is an instructional assistant. He'd especially like to thank his daughters, Molly and Natalie, for reading *Knuffle Bunny* almost ten years ago and sparking Matt's thinking about young readers.

Finally, we owe everything to the many, many children over the years who have never failed to teach us, to inspire us, and to amaze us.

INTRODUCTION

I believe that education, therefore, is a process
of living and not a preparation for future living.
—JOHN DEWEY (1887)

All children start their school careers with
sparkling imaginations, fertile minds, and a
willingness to take risks with what they think.
—SIR KEN ROBINSON (2009)

Over the years, we've watched young children interact enthusiastically with books they can't yet decode. We've seen children lie side by side on carpet swatches, rushing to be the first to name the figures on the pages of the newest Star Wars Lego book. We've listened to children read (in approximated ways) a favorite picture book that has been read to them at least a hundred times by grown-ups at home and in school. We've observed children read information books by naming what they see in the pictures. We've witnessed hundreds of children create stories, complete with dialogue and narration, based only on their interpretations of the illustrations in picture books they've never seen before.

As we observe children read books before they can read conventionally, we grow more and more fascinated by what we see. We wonder what children think about about as they make their merry way through the pages. How do they figure out how to read in these ways? What do they do to make sense of what they are looking at? What do they believe about reading? About themselves as readers? How can children's identities as readers and interest in books be strengthened and extended? What might this mean in classrooms?

These questions have been the focus of many of our conversations over the years, and our ongoing curiosity about what readers do before they can read the words turned into an inquiry to find out. We collected videos of young children interacting with books and analyzed what we observed. We talked to teachers and to parents about what they saw their children doing with books at home. Our curiosity and inquiry became the catalyst for writing this book together.

We arrived at our collaboration from slightly different pathways. Kathy brings her experience with teaching readers, whereas much of Matt's work has been concentrated on supporting writers. Kathy's work focuses heavily on children's comprehension and engagement in reading, while Matt centers much of his work on composition and engagement in writing. But what inititally brought us together (aside from long discussions about our own children, the brilliance of *The Wire*, and our baseball allegiances) is our fascination with children's thinking. We share a deep passion for nurturing intellectual development and joyful engagement as children both comprehend and compose text.

We also share a concern about some of the contemporary priorities of education, namely the changing notion of early childhood teaching and learning in these days of high-stakes testing, constant data collection, and the singular pursuit of the race to the top. We worry about the consequences when kindergarten is viewed primarily as a step toward college and career readiness. We worry when children in preschool spend ever-larger portions of their day doing worksheets at their seats. In schools across the country, we encounter teachers and children who are in a constant state of getting ready for the next big test within school cultures characterized by heightened anxiety.

With regard to early literacy, specifically, we frequently see instruction that is focused on moving young children to the next text levels as fast as possible, and whether children enjoy reading or fall in love with books or develop habits that will benefit them throughout their lives becomes an afterthought, not a priority. Early childhood teachers are struggling to acclimate to the intensity of academic demands while also tending to the humanity of their children.

There is a top-down sensibility at work in which the pressures and expectations for older students have been pushed down in ways that profoundly affect the school days of our youngest children. In many places, the big work for little children has become simply to get ready for the challenges of the next grade or to prepare for some upcoming assessment. The problem, we see, is that readiness, itself, has become the goal. We believe that if we provide rich learning opportunities by meeting children where they are and teaching them in a way that is ambitious but also considerate of childhood, readiness will be the by-product.

To be clear, we're not against readiness per se. We're not arguing for unpreparedness. No teacher would ever say she wasn't concerned about whether or not her students were ready for the challenges of the next grade. No teacher would be satisfied if his children weren't ready to handle upcoming work. We don't have an issue with the idea of being ready. Instead, we're concerned when readiness becomes the singular goal.

The fetish around readiness leads us to actions and expectations in classrooms that may not match the children in front of us and may not ultimately be in their best interests. For example, when children are limited only to just-right leveled texts and word-solving instruction at earlier and earlier ages, they may develop decoding skills at the expense of meaning-making dispositions and a sense of playfulness with books. When three-year-olds are taught letter formation and pencil grip, it's at the expense of other motor skill–building opportunities that might be more aligned with the needs and interests of those three-year-olds. When we reduce recess time to increase instructional time, we may also increase children's distractedness and inability to focus. When we teach reading as if the only objective is to climb levels, we're inadvertently creating reading identity issues among those children who aren't yet reading the hardest books.

Our response to this emphasis on readiness as the goal is simply this: children are always ready for something, and our most effective teaching meets them where they are and nudges them toward what might be next. Therefore, in this book, we're advocating for supporting young children's reading in ways that nurture their healthy reading identities, that fosters an attraction toward texts and a love for reading, and that teaches them how to make meaning in any text they choose, whether or not they can read the words. It's our intention to first honor and then build upon the sophisticated thinking that children do in books even before they begin to read conventionally.

How This Book Works

Before exploring strategies for supporting readers, we want to make the case for why approximated reading matters. Throughout the book, we remind readers that we aren't diminishing the importance of conventional reading. Rather, we are expanding a view of reading to include and support all readers, regardless of how they are making meaning. Chapter 1 provides an overview and rationale for why it's important to support childrens' meaning-making dispositions and identities as readers before they can even read the words.

In Chapters 2 through 6, we examine what children do as they read familiar, unfamiliar, and informational texts and why experiences with all of these types of texts are important. We also offer specific ideas for nurturing and supporting children's thinking during reading conferences. In Chapter 7, we deal with issues of independence, and we suggest ways that we can help children become more self-initated and engaged when they read any kind of book.

In Chapters 8 and 9, we consider classroom implications for this type of work, specifically in preschool, kindergarten, and first grade. We provide suggestions for kinds of structures, opportunities, and instruction that teachers and caregivers can provide to help young children do increasingly more sophisticated and intentional meaning-making work. In Chapter 10, we take a wide-angled look at what a year of instructional support for meaning making and identity building might look like. Finally, in Chapter 11, we offer some suggestions for turning the ideas in this book into plans of action.

Understanding Through Seeing: The Importance of Video Clips

We had the joy of reading with so many young children, and we wanted their presence to infuse our book. We began by including transcripts, but words on the page never truly captured Neve's amazement as she read her horse book or Natalie's persistence in turning each and every page of *Knuffle Bunny*. So instead of only transcripts or descriptions of what we observed, we've included links to videos of children reading familiar, unfamiliar, and informational books and clips of teachers leading lessons and sitting beside children in conferences.

You will want to watch these clips as they come up while you read because the text and the videos are dependent on one another for context. We found it difficult to represent in a written transcript everything that you can watch unfold in a video. Also, the videos provide space for differentiation: we trust that you'll notice things in the videos that we didn't and that the clips will bring to mind your own children's interactions with books.

You may notice that in some clips you can't see the book the child is reading because we weren't able to secure permission from the publisher to show the book in the video. In any case, the focus of these video clips is not on which particular book the child is reading, but instead it's about how that child is interacting with the book.

We've provided a couple of ways for you to access the clips while you're reading:

1. For each clip there is a QR code that looks like this: You can scan the code with a free app you can download to your cell phone or tablet. When you scan the code it will take you to the specific video clip.

2. You can find the menu for all of the clips at: https://heinemann.com /IAmReading. Whenever you come across a link in the text, just go to this home page and select the clip you want corresponding to the clip number. It will help to bookmark the home page on your browser so you can access it quickly.

Whichever method you choose, our intention is for the videos to provide vivid examples of children reading familiar, unfamiliar, and informational books in approximated ways and to show how teachers can support young readers as they do this work.

It is our hope that children at any age identify themselves as readers, with abilities and strategies to make meaning in every text they encounter. That identity begins when they look through their first board book, and it continues to evolve throughout adulthood. Our biggest desire is that this book will expand teachers' and parents' views of what it means to be a reader, and as result, the reading lives of children will be consistently and intentionally nurtured and nudged both at school and at home.

CHAPTER 1

Reading or Not— Here We Come!

A few years ago, a pre-dawn channel surfer might have caught the info-mercial for *Your Baby Can Read*, an early childhood reading program. This infomercial featured a medley of very young children reading words from flashcards and texts. In our hazy recollection, it went something like this: the camera would zoom in on a sweet-faced child and her parent, who was sitting nearby holding up flashcards. The child would gaze at the cards for a millisecond before calling out, "Pathogen," "Irony," "Calculation." (We admit those may not have been the *actual* flashcard words, but you get the point.)

As the infomercial went on, the toddlers changed to preschool-age children. A four-year-old read aloud from *Charlotte's Web* or some equally worthy book, while an adult looked on adoringly. Did the child read this beloved text with accuracy? Check. Fluency? Absolutely. Comprehension? Probably not, but who knows, and besides, does it really matter? That little child could read the words in *Charlotte's Web*!

At the end of the infomercial, a parent made a breathless testimonial about the effectiveness of the Your Baby Can Read! program. At this point, any viewer with young children or anyone who even knew young children would need to muster all of his or her willpower to refrain from calling the toll-free number to place an order. The commercial was that good!

The Your Baby Can Read! Company was successfully selling a vision of reading, a $200 vision, to hopeful "parents and grandparents of children aged three months to five years old" (Federal Trade Commission 2012). Alas, the old saying "too good to be true" proved to be applicable. The Federal Trade Commission filed a complaint against the Your Baby Can Read Company for false advertising and charged the product's creator with making "deceptive expert endorsements" (Federal Trade Commission 2012). After making more than $185 million in profits, the Your Baby Can Read! Company went out of business.

Although this reading program may have been based on bad reading science and misleading promises, it was presented to the public in a seductive infomercial that appealed to adults' loving impulses to do right by their children. And even though Your Baby Can Read! was declared a failed method for accelerating young children's abilities to read, it effectively perpetuated some narrow ideas about reading. First, it suggested that reading is all about decoding and that a child who decodes is a full-fledged, complete reader. Second, it promoted the idea that the earlier a child decodes text, the more successful the child will be in school and in life. Third, it implied that children learn to read most efficiently and effectively through flashcards and drills and that reading a real book is only the product of learning to read, not part of the process of learning to read.

The Rush to Read the Words

We acknowledge that there are precocious four-year-olds who decode text legitimately. Some children do walk in on the first day of preschool already able to read the words in Little Bear or Henry and Mudge books. Many first-grade teachers have had at least one child begin the school year claiming to have read a Harry Potter book or something of that heft over the summer. It's certainly quite possible for a child to be a very early decoder, and we can't help but look on in amazement when this is the case. After all, decoding the words is the flashy face of reading. It's the grand facade, the sparkly outer layer, the fondant frosting. Because decoding words is the part of reading we can see and hear instantly and on demand, parents and educators often view the ability to decode early as a sign that their young child or student will be better than fine.

Over the last several years, school systems have been decreasing the age at which they expect children to read conventionally. At home, many families are hooked on phonics before their children are freed from diapers. New parents download literacy apps for their devices, and very young children sit still in car seats and quietly in restaurants, their little fingers swishing across touch screens as they bring together parts of compound words or match letters to sounds. It has become a sign of good parenting to front-load young children's reading lives with educational games, high-priced kits, leveled books, and literacy apps. Although these well-marketed products are purchased with good intentions and high hopes, research suggests that the most helpful ways parents can support young children's literacy are to talk with and read to their children. This kind of support is a crucial factor in long-term school success and engagement. Although we've written this book with classroom teachers in mind, we hope that many of the suggestions and ideas we've included will give parents productive ways to nurture their children's literacy development at home.

Meanwhile, at school, in preschool and kindergarten classrooms, teachers are being encouraged (or forced) to increase the instructional emphasis and time spent on teaching young children to decode words earlier than ever. Many prekindergarten classrooms dedicate ever-larger portions of wall space to word walls and literacy anchor charts while also devoting more time to formal reading instruction. In kindergarten, the time for imaginary play and the space for block areas have given way to space for reading nooks and time for literacy blocks. If you look inside many early childhood classrooms, it might be hard to tell the difference between a pre-K space and a kindergarten room, and, meanwhile, the lines have certainly been blurred between kindergarten and first grade over the last several years.

In truth, most of these monumental changes in the environments and expectations of early childhood classrooms haven't been teacher-driven. A vast majority of pre-K and kindergarten teachers we meet mourn the loss of adequate recess time and play opportunities. We hear story upon story of early childhood teachers who feel pressure to ramp up academic work to meet constantly rising expectations at the expense of authentic inquiry and play. These profound changes to early childhood classrooms have largely come from influences outside of and unfamiliar with early childhood research and practice.

Although we accelerate expectations for our youngest children, many other countries still wait to begin formal reading instruction until children are six or seven years old. Schools in Sweden, for example, wait until children are seven before formal reading instruction begins, and Sweden has one of the highest literacy rates in the world (Teaching Channel 2014). Waiting to begin formal reading instruction until children were in first grade used to be typical in the United States, as well. These days, it's the norm for even preschool programs to tout their academic rigor by assuring prospective parents that there's time each day devoted to formal reading instruction.

Back in 2000 (which is actually *not that long ago*), the ability to read a text at Fountas & Pinnell Level B was a typical end-of-the-year grade-level expectation for kindergarten. Then the "level-creep" phenomenon began. It started slowly. In many districts, the year-end

> *In our rush to get children decoding text and reaching quantifiable reading benchmarks at earlier and earlier ages, we miss out on all the other real and important reading, thinking, and talking work and play that young children do as they turn the pages of books. And children miss out on time to establish playful, intentional, self-initiated ways to interact with texts.*

kindergarten grade-level expectation rose to Fountas & Pinnell Levels C or D as educators acknowledged the very real issue of summer reading loss (Allington and McGill-Frazen 2012). Recently, we worked in a school where the end-of-the-year expectation in kindergarten was for children to read a Fountas & Pinnell Level F, and the preschool end-of-the-year expectation was that all of the children will read conventionally! Sight word acquisition expectations have also increased. In 2000, a kindergartener who could read and write twenty-five sight words was considered fine. These days, the amount of sight words kindergartners need to know has tripled in many places. In less than fifteen years, the end-of-year academic expectations for kindergartners have risen sharply.

There are many reasons for this. Research on summer reading loss shows that young children can slip back a level or two over the summer. Although this is a research-based rationale for raising end-of-year expectations, it isn't the only catalyst for such steep level creep. The contemporary emphasis on (or obsession with) college and career readiness has made its way into kindergarten and pre-K classrooms. The rationale is that the standards and expectations have been raised so much for twelfth graders, so we have to also raise them much higher all the way down to early childhood. Due to the tyranny of these priorities to get younger kids reading faster in the name of college and career readiness, red flags go up when our youngest school-aged children don't decode words or achieve a designated reading level per a pacing calendar that's sped up drastically in the past fifteen years.

Of course, some kindergarten children can easily reach or exceed these modern expectations, but a great many children (and teachers) may find them extraordinarily challenging or unattainable. In many cases, kindergarten children's reading levels may not rise as quickly or as easily as the accelerated expectations demand, but their frustration levels certainly do! These days, it's not unusual to call meetings with parents, draw up paperwork, schedule resource room teachers, and sound the alarms when a child isn't reading at a particular level of proficiency within the first month of school.

We're all caught in the hurry-scurry rush to get children reading conventionally, yet we know that reading involves much more than cracking the code and figuring out the words in a book. After all, a five- or six-year-old decoding *Harry Potter* books is not the same as a thirteen-year-old *reading* Harry Potter books. Robust and well-rounded reading is the interplay among the abilities to decode print, read it with fluency, and make meaning of it all. Reading is the elegant orchestration of macro and micro skills and strategies. The act of reading is swaddled in purpose, schema, response, and so many other things. And developing an identity as a reader and the motivation to read involves so much more than reading levels, word counts, fluency rates, and assessments.

A consequence of rushing toward ever-higher reading levels in the early years is that we fail to see all of the wonders and charm, as well as the strategy use and high-level thinking, that are part of children's preconventional "reading magic," to use Mem Fox's sweet phrase. In our rush to get children decoding text and reaching quantifiable reading benchmarks at earlier and earlier ages, we miss out on all the other real and important reading, thinking, and talking work and play that young children do as they turn the pages of books. And children miss out on time to establish playful, intentional, self-initiated ways to interact with texts.

It is our belief that when the focus of young children's interactions with texts prioritizes decoding with accuracy and reaching higher reading levels at younger ages, we are yanking children into the world of reading rather than welcoming them. We are pushing them, rather than nudging them. As an alternative, we propose an approach to working with our youngest children in ways that nurture their reading intentions. We propose helping young children develop healthy, functional reader identities; finding ways to increase their engagement with books; and teaching strategies to hone their meaning-making and problem-solving abilities.

What Does Real Reading Look Like?

Recently a YouTube video went viral even though it didn't feature anthropomorphized cats or talking dogs. This particular video featured two young sisters, Zoe and Maddie, singing "Let It Go," the ubiquitous song from the Disney movie, *Frozen*. In the video, Zoe and Maddie stand tall at microphones wearing professional-looking headphones, singing as if they were at a studio recording session. Zoe and Maddie performed a song they had likely heard dozens of times and had memorized, and anyone who watches the video would say that these girls are singing their little hearts out. They are charming and unself-conscious, and there's no wonder that millions of people have viewed their video.

Let's imagine this going another way. What if the video featured Zoe and Maddie reading a picture book, say a Piggie and Elephant book, that had been read aloud to them dozens of times and that they knew by heart? What if Zoe and Maddie read this Piggie and Elephant book aloud the same way they sang "Let It Go," unself-consciously, charmingly, accurately, with vocal intonations, facial expressions, and gestures? Would we say they were reading Piggie and Elephant, or would we say they had just memorized it? Would we view their work as reading or not?

Although we don't have a video of Zoe and Maddie reading a book, we invite you to watch Matt's daughter, then two-and-a-half-year old Natalie, interact with *Knuffle Bunny*, a picture book that her parents read to her and her twin sister Molly many, many times. As you watch, please consider these questions, "What is Natalie doing? Is Natalie reading or is she 'reading'?"

Clip 1.1 *Natalie Reads* **Knuffle Bunny** *(Familiar Book)*
http://smarturl.it/Clip1.1

Bookmark https://heinemann .com/IAmReading to easily access a menu of the video clips.

Judging from the comments posted to the Zoe and Maddie's "Let It Go" video, most people view what they are doing as real singing yet, at first glance, most people don't think what Natalie is doing with *Knuffle Bunny* is real reading. Yet in both videos, the children are interacting with a text (a song in one and a picture book in another) that they know by heart. In both videos, the children are not decoding the text. Zoe and Maddie aren't sight-reading the sheet music or lyrics as they sing, nor is Natalie attending to the print. In both videos, the children rely largely upon what they know of the text from having heard it many times before, although all three of the children add their own quirky, individual twists. In both videos, the children imitate what they've seen and heard to look and sound like their images of a singer or a reader.

Even though the children in these videos are approaching the tasks of singing "Let It Go" and reading *Knuffle Bunny* in very similar ways, viewers have different perceptions about what they are doing. Zoe and Maddie are singing, while Natalie is "reading." The "reading" (imagine air quotes around that word) that Natalie is doing with *Knuffle Bunny* requires qualification—Natalie is reading from memory. Natalie is pretend-reading. Natalie isn't really *reading Knuffle Bunny*. Because Natalie's isn't actually decoding the text, it's hard for many viewers to see what she's doing as reading.

LOOKING THROUGH THE CUTE LENS

What viewers see as they watch Natalie's interaction with *Knuffle Bunny* is dependent on the lens with which they watch. One way we can view Natalie is through the Cute Lens. As we watch with the Cute Lens, we appreciate the many charms of the moment, from Natalie's footie jammies to her sweetly enthusiastic toddler voice. We love the way she pronounces *Knuffle Bunny*. If she were your child, you'd likely add her way of saying *Knuffle Bunny* to your family lore of childhood pronunciations or malapropisms, to be dusted off and remembered nostalgically when the kids are older.

Through the Cute Lens, we love the expression of distress Natalie makes when Trixie realizes that her beloved Knuffle Bunny is gone. We might even ask Natalie to read *Knuffle Bunny* to visiting relatives, just so they can enjoy how darn cute she is when she makes her Knuffle Bunny distress face.

The Cute Lens leads us to take pictures or record videos of Natalie sitting next to her crib in her fleece footie pajamas reading her favorite book because we want to remember. We want to stop time and capture this moment of little Natalie reading her current favorite book because we understand that these times in our child's lives are fleeting and unique.

OBSERVING WITH A NO BIG DEAL LENS

Another lens with which to watch Natalie is the No Big Deal Lens. When viewing through this lens, Natalie's interaction with *Knuffle Bunny* is nothing special because she knows the book by heart. "We've read it to her before bed for the last six months," a parent might say. "She has just memorized the story," another parent might think, which suggests that Natalie is simply parroting an adult. It's no big deal. In many cases, when children are quietly and safely occupied by reading familiar books to themselves, parents may use these moments to take care of their own business or tasks, simply because what their child is doing is no big deal.

The Cute Lens and the No Big Deal Lens are not just ways for parents and caregivers to view children. Teachers observe children through these lenses, too. If Natalie were in an early childhood classroom sitting beside a sand table rather than her crib and wearing striped tights rather than footie pajamas, a teacher might view her interaction with *Knuffle Bunny* through either the Cute or the No Big Deal Lens. A teacher might observe for a moment and store up this anecdote until dismissal time when she shares it with Natalie's parent. Alternatively, the teacher might sit beside Natalie briefly as she reads *Knuffle Bunny* and tell her, "Good job!" before moving along to another child.

Viewing young children through the Cute Lens or the No Big Deal Lens may be our default lenses. It's important to note that we don't think there is anything inherently wrong with these lenses, and the Cute Lens, in particular, is one that families and educators should have on hand. After all, appreciating the charms of a child at work or play is a loving way to "see" that child. Unfortunately, overreliance on these lenses can have a downside. They narrow our view of the child because when we focus on the cute aspects or undervalue the child's work or play, we may end up missing the significance of what a child is doing in any given moment.

SEEING THROUGH THE READING LENS

So how else might we view Natalie and *Knuffle Bunny* so that we notice more than what's cute? We can watch her through a Reading Lens. The Reading Lens gives us the depth perception to go beneath the surface of the scene and enables us to observe what Natalie may feel, believe, and know about reading. This lens can allow us to begin to understand children's relationships to reading and to books while also revealing ways we can support them.

The video opens with Matt asking Natalie, "Can you read this? What's that book called?" Natalie responds with an enthusiastic, "Knuffle Bunny!" and gets right to business as she opens the book without hesitation. Natalie doesn't request that her dad sidle up next to her to read to her, nor does she respond, "You read!" Of course, there are many variables at work, from the amount that her family reads to her to how many times she's heard *Knuffle Bunny*, from her unique personality to her comfort level in the situation. Perhaps in another setting with another text, Natalie may not have been as confident and ready, but this particular event shows us that she can have a comfortable relationship with books and confidence in her ability to read, especially with familiar books.

Very soon after opening the book, Natalie issues an invitation to Molly, her twin sister (0:07), to read the book with her. Molly denies the invitation and scoots off to get another book. Unbothered, Natalie begins to read. When viewed through the Reading Lens, we see that Natalie already understands that reading can be a social activity and that a reading experience can be shared, or not. The "or not" moment, when Molly heads away and Natalie maintains her focus on *Knuffle Bunny*, suggests that Natalie is also very comfortable sitting by herself with a book. Natalie intends to read this particular book regardless of whether or not her sister wants to join her.

As Natalie begins to read, she points to the action on the page and narrates it, saying something like, "They go in the park." She says this twice, matching the illustration to her version of the text. Elizabeth Sulzby would call this following the action in a picture governed attempt (Sulzby 1985), and this is one way young children read familiar books without being attentive to the print.

Natalie turns the pages and at a point, says something unclear, and her dad asks, "They're going to the Laundromat?" (0:32). In that situation, Natalie is accessing the vocabulary of the text, trying to say *Laundromat*, and Natalie's dad naturally supports her language development and vocabulary acquisition without breaking the world of the story.

After Trixie and her dad arrive at the Laundromat, Natalie turns the page and twice exclaims, "Knuffle Bunny!" (0:37) and points to the stuffed animal stuck in the washing machine. Her vigorous exclamation of his name when she locates him in the washing machine shows that Natalie understands that Trixie doesn't realize her beloved stuffed animal is lost. Her voice expresses a sense of tension in that part of the story.

Next, Natalie turns the page again and says, "Let's go home, Dad," giving voice to Trixie. So far, on three pages where she paused, Natalie does three completely different things as a reader:

- She narrates action on the page.
- She locates and identifies a character with a vocal intonation that suggests she's holding on to the meaning of the story.
- She "embodies" the character by giving the character voice or approximating the dialogue in her retelling.

In addition to highlighting all of the ways Natalie makes meaning and connects the illustrations with her schema of how the story goes, the Reading Lens allows us to also observe the many early reading behaviors and book-handling skills Natalie has acquired.

When we watch young children like Natalie through a Reading Lens, we are struck by just how much reading work they're doing and how many skills and strategies they're presenting before they read one word conventionally. For many reasons, we realize that when viewed through a Reading Lens, Natalie's interaction with this text is so much deeper than cute and so much more significant than "no big deal."

An Enriched and Inclusive Definition of Reading

The word *read* and its variations are used in a variety of expressions and idioms that have nothing to do with figuring out the words on a page. For example:

"I read the room when I walked in to the meeting. I knew things were tense."
"Her face was so easy to read. She was clearly surprised."
"Let me get a read on the situation, and I'll let you know what we should do."
"I could read between the lines. I knew he was going to quit."
"Do you read me?"

In all of these cases, the word *read* is used to express an act of understanding or moment of meaning making. To read anything—a face, a room, a text—is to make meaning. When we read, whether it's a book or a person or a situation, our primary intention is to understand.

When it comes to reading texts or reading instruction, there are many "official" definitions, depending on the background of whom you ask. A neurologist might define the act of reading as a complex function of the central nervous system, and a brain researcher might define reading in part as the lateralization of brain function. An elementary school teacher might define reading as the ability to decode text with accuracy, fluency, and comprehension. A high school teacher might say that reading is largely the ability to analyze and interpret texts. A survey of the literature of so many of our reading heroes, from the Goodmans to Calkins, from Keene to Smith, from Cambourne to Clay, Harvey to Gallagher, Santman to Kittle, Beers to Allington, Fountas to Pinnell, Rosenblatt to Miller, Serravallo to the Sisters, Newkirk to Bomer, and so on reveals many other definitions—some poetic, some clinical.

Even though there are already many definitions to answer the question "What is reading?" we'd like to throw another one into the mix. After watching many young children interact with books, we've come up with this response:

> Reading is an interaction with a text during which the reader uses a variety of resources within the text (i.e., words, pictures, graphic elements, etc.) and within themselves (schema, skills, strategies) to make meaning.

When we consider this definition, we realize that even before children decode words, they are reading texts. They are readers. As we watch Natalie read *Knuffle Bunny*, we see a confident reader who is making meaning in a text. We watch as she uses the pictures to help anchor her to the story. We see how she modulates her voice to express the tension and emotion experienced by the characters. We notice how many functional reading habits she already has in place. According to our definition, Natalie is reading, even though she's not yet reading the words in the text.

To be fair, we acknowledge that some people might watch the video and say, "Nope, that's not real reading." We can understand that position; however, our response would be to ask, "What would she need to do differently to be seen as a real reader?"

To be considered a real reader, would Natalie need to decode words? If so, that leads to other questions. If she needs to decode words to be really reading, what would her accuracy rate need to be? Well, Natalie is little, so maybe she needs to decode only some of the words. What's the cutoff? If she needs to decode only some of the words, which ones? The sight words? What if Natalie could decode some or all of the words, but she didn't understand what the text said? Would that be real reading?

At this point, some people might say, "Well, it's not so black and white," and they might feel more comfortable if we put qualifying language here. Instead of saying that Natalie is a reader, it might be easier to say that Natalie is a pre-emergent reader or a beginning reader, or an approximating reader. This qualifying language allows us to hedge our bets a bit: "Well, she's sorta kinda reading, in a way."

Although we understand the inclination to add qualifying language, we don't feel it's always necessary or helpful. We believe that when young children are somewhere on the reading (or writing) continuum, it's in their best interests (and ours) to view them as readers (or writers) and to support their growth from wherever they are on the continuum (Ray and Glover 2008).

When we adults envision what children are doing as real reading, we interact with them differently and see the richness in what they are doing. When children envision what they are doing as real reading, they see themselves differently.

When we adults envision what children are doing as real reading, we interact with them differently and see the richness in what they are doing. When children envision what they are doing as real reading, they see themselves differently. This is win-win. As we sit down next to our youngest children and see them as readers, we can offer support and nudges to grow as people who are willing to explore books and take on challenges.

As children interact with any kind of text, from fiction to informational and every genre in between, from books they know and love to books they never seen before, we've learned that *prior to decoding*, young children:

- strive to make meaning, using a wide range of comprehension skills and strategies
- try to read with fluency, smoothly and expressively
- acquire vocabulary and extend their oral language
- utilize the social component of reading to their advantage
- use text features (i.e., pictures, graphic elements) to figure out tricky parts
- form their reading identities
- respond to texts through talk and play

Children's preconventional reading experiences with text serve an important role in shaping their reading strengths, reading identities, and reading attitudes. We believe that educators and caregivers have so much to offer children at this precious and fleeting time when we stay in this moment with them, rather than moving them quickly toward reading the words conventionally.

Our intentions for writing this book are many, but one of our biggest hopes is that we can help you see and value all of the powerful work children do as readers even before we can score their accuracy rate or assess their fluency according to a rubric. We want to share a more expansive view of what it means to be a young reader, and we will offer ideas and suggestions for nudging children toward conventional reading in ways that celebrate, rather than negate, all of the playful approaches and joyful engagement they bring to texts.

By sharing the stories of young children engaging deeply with texts, observing them as they use sophisticated comprehension strategies, watching as they develop positive reading identities—all before they begin to read the words—we hope to inspire ideas for ways to identify and support all of the amazing reading work young children do that doesn't involve an emphasis on word solving. We hope to shine a light on and give you the lenses to see the wonderful and vast world of reading that exists even before decoding begins.

CHAPTER 2

I Know This One! Reading Familiar Picture Books

Children are attracted to the familiar. Many kids could happily eat the same food at every meal. Children can be effusive and outgoing around familiar adults but hesitant and tentative toward those they've just met. Lots of kids go through stages when they demand to wear the same clothes day after day after day. Before bedtime, they'll search for books that they know well and ask their caregiver to read them over and over and over. In most cases, children gravitate toward the comfort of familiarity.

We acknowledge that outside the world of childhood and beyond the walls of early childhood classrooms, familiarity has a fraught reputation. It's not as trendy as innovation nor as hip as novelty. There's even a common saying, "Familiarity breeds contempt," that puts a negative frame on the familiar. Despite this, there are many positive attributes of familiarity and potential opportunities in the world of the familiar, especially with regard to familiar reading, so say the authors of this book—who would eat peanut-butter-and-jelly sandwiches every day (Kathy) and French toast every morning (Matt).

Because young children tend to choose to read familiar books both at home and in the classroom, we asked ourselves two questions:

1. What are children doing and thinking about when they reread well-loved and familiar books?

2. How can we support children's reading growth and identities as they interact with well-loved and familiar books?

Many adults can think back fondly on a book they knew by heart when they were little. Matt looks back and recalls his *Go. Dog. Go!* glory days, and Kathy waxes nostalgic for *The Little Brute Family,* books they heard and read a thousand times as children. These books, well-worn and well-loved, and the interactions with the grown-ups who read them aloud made an important impression in their lives. In general, the books that were read over and over to us and that we chose to revisit in our childhoods serve as the gateway texts leading to our lifelong desire to read and to fill our homes with books.

Typically, the first reading act that's initiated by a child is the request for someone to read aloud a familiar favorite book. Young children do this in many different ways. Ten-month-old Zoey responds physically to books she knows and loves. She adjusts herself into a just-so reading position on her mom's lap, which is different than her "pat-a-cake" position or her "I'm so sleepy" position. Zoey's breathing quickens, she babbles joyfully, and she gestures excitedly as her mom rereads *Good Night, Gorilla*, her favorite little board book.

With determination, two-year-old Will steps over toys and around the family dog to squat in front of the basket of books on the floor next to the window. He paws through it, looking for *The Napping House*. He finds it. Crisis averted. Will carries the book and his blanket over to his dad, signaling that it's both naptime *and* storytime.

Children's repeated requests for adults to read and reread favorite books can be beautifully exasperating. We think to ourselves, "No! Not *The Wheels on the Bus* again" while we rouse up some energy to, in fact, read it again. Meanwhile, our children sit beside us, eagerly pointing out familiar characters, paraphrasing bits of the tune, and mimicking our singsong intonation as we read the text. For these children and so many others, familiarity breeds enthusiasm.

Our young students enter their classrooms on the first few days of school looking for something, anything, that will help them feel comfortable in their new world. As Mario's eyes anxiously pan his kindergarten classroom on the first day of school, he notices that the teacher has the exact same Piggie and Elephant book that he has at home. Mario pulls his mom over to the classroom library and asks her to read it. When Livvy, a third grader, spots a tattered copy of *The Snowy Day* in a box of books in the classroom closet, she grabs it and gushes to her teacher, "I read this book when I was little!" For these children, familiarity breeds comfort.

Sometimes when caregivers or teachers read aloud a book over and over to a child, the child's familiarity with the text can turn her into a rigid taskmaster. The sweet and gentle bedtime reading routine can turn bad quickly if Kira's dad dares to veer from what she expects to hear on each turn of the page of *Rollercoaster*. If Grandma doesn't use the same rising intonation voice as mom when she reads aloud this month's favorite, *Where Is the Green Sheep?*, Raymond is likely to demand that Grandma start over and "read it good." When a couple of kindergartners sit together to read *Scaredy Squirrel*, they do not hesitate to correct each other if the book isn't being read "the right way." For these kids, familiarity breeds confidence.

For these reasons, we would like to revise the expression, "Familiarity breeds contempt," to "Familiarity breeds comfort, enthusiasm, and confidence." Put another way with young learners in mind, we could say the comfort of familiarity creates opportunities to activate schema and meaning-making strategies. The enthusiasm that familiarity invites increases engagement. The confidence that's bred by familiarity encourages a sense of agency (Johnston 2004). How fortunate for early childhood educators and for young children's caregivers that the benefits of familiarity also contain necessary conditions for healthy learning!

In this chapter, we suggest that providing opportunities for young children to regularly read familiar texts is important for well-rounded reading development, vital for their joyful engagement with texts, and crucial for helping children to develop a growth mind-set (Dweck 2007) toward their reading and toward themselves as readers.

We want to be clear that this chapter about children's interactions with familiar books is written under the influence of the work of Marie Clay and Elizabeth Sulzby. They've informed so much of our thinking, especially with respect to the valuable work children do when they read books they know so well.

Benefits of Rereading Familiar Books

There is a continuum of familiarity, and it actually begins with unfamiliarity (Figure 2.1). Unfamiliarity with a book may range from never having seen the text before to recognizing the cover but not knowing what's inside on the pages.

The next degree of familiarity is when a child knows something about a particular book, even though it has never been read aloud to the child. For example, four-year-old Laura knows several Olivia books really well because they've been read aloud to her both at home

Text Familiarity Continuum

Unfamiliar	Somewhat Familiar	Securely Familiar	Very Familiar
I've seen the text before, but nobody has ever read it to me. *Or* I haven't seen this one yet.	I know something about this text just because something about it is familiar. I know the main character, the series, or the story line (i.e., a new version of Little Red Riding Hood). Nobody has read this particular book to me, though.	I have heard this text before at least once, and I know how it goes.	I've heard this text a lot of times, at home, in school, or at both places, and I know it well.

Figure 2.1

and in her preschool classroom. As a result, Laura knows Olivia, the character, and she has schema for how Olivia tends to act and for how these books tend to go. Even so, Laura isn't familiar with a particular book, *Olivia Forms a Band,* because nobody has read it to her before. Therefore, we call this type of text a "somewhat familiar" book.

When a book has been read aloud to a child at least once and the child has listened and looked attentively at the text, we consider that book to be in the securely familiar category. The child knows how the book goes. Once the book has been read to the child over and over again, however, we consider that to take on another degree of familiarity—very familiar. Books in the very familiar category are those that the child has heard more than several times.

It's worth noting that we have expanded the breadth of familiar books in a slight point of departure from (not a critique of) the work of Elizabeth Sulzby and the Kindergarten Literacy Project. We understand that in the KLP approach, books are made familiar by the teacher. Teachers select certain picture books according to certain criteria that will become the students' "familiar" books. Teachers read these books aloud to their students multiple times before making them available to children (Sulzby 1985).

In contrast, we've broadened the scope of books we're considering to be familiar texts to include texts that haven't necessarily been chosen by the teacher nor read only by the teacher. Children interact with texts beyond the school walls, so what constitutes a "familiar" book is often a text read outside the context of the classroom. One of our intentions in our research was to figure out how to support children as they read *any* familiar book, not just the ones the teacher selects according to certain criteria and then reads aloud several times to the class.

For the purposes of supporting young readers as they read familiar books, we will look most closely at children's interactions with books that are either securely familiar or very familiar, whether or not the teacher selected them and read them aloud already to the class.

At this point, before we go on in the chapter, we invite you to take a moment to watch a video clip of Alex reading *Chicka Chicka Boom Boom*. This is a book he knows well because it has been read aloud to him many times. Here are some questions to consider as you watch:

1. What might Alex's words and actions reveal about his ideas of what it means to read?
2. What does Alex do and say as he reads that help him make meaning?
3. What do you notice about Alex's affect and engagement as he reads?
4. How much of Alex's reading is memorized?

Clip 2.1 *Alex Reads* Chicka Chicka Boom Boom *(Familiar)*
http://smarturl.it/Clip2.1

A teacher who watches Alex read *Chicka Chicka Boom Boom* may very well say, "I knew he could pretend-read that one. He's heard it so many times." Often, when we catch a moment with a child who is reading a very familiar book, we tend to observe briefly, offer praise, and move along. There doesn't seem to be an opening for a teaching and learning interaction because the child knows the book so well.

Because they know the books so well, children's interactions with familiar texts tend to be undervalued and viewed through the No Big Deal Lens. "Someone has read it aloud to him at least five hundred times, so of course he can read it. I'd be worried if he couldn't!" or "He's not really reading it; he's memorized it!" are typical reactions adults might have as they watch a child read a book they know really well.

With our Cute Lenses, we appreciate the charm of Alex reading his beloved books, and with our No Big Deal lens, we might play down the significance of the reading event. It is with our Reading Lens, however, that we begin to realize all of the behind-the-scenes thinking work that Alex is doing, even though he has heard the book no less than five hundred times and may even have it memorized.

Marie Clay might have called Alex's reading of *Chicka Chicka Boom Boom* a version of "roaming around in the known." Clay wrote that "confidence, ease, flexibility, and with luck, discovery" are benefits for the learner when they are working within the familiar (Clay 2005). When we watch Alex and other children roam around in the known within the worlds of these very familiar texts, we, as educators, or we, as caregivers, also benefit. We observe what they know to do on their own, what they understand about reading, and what they're not quite doing yet. This is invaluable information because it allows us to calibrate our instruction and fine-tune our interactions in a personal and responsive way.

As we watch Alex read *Chicka Chicka Boom Boom*, we notice several things (Figure 2.2) that indicate learning benefits for children when they have frequent opportunities to re-read books that they know and love. When we observe children as they "roam around in the known," we realize that they use a number of meaning-making strategies to help them move through even the most familiar books. Because they are not decoding, children call upon and use their oral language stores to retrieve words and phrases. They develop confidence and identity as readers. Perhaps most importantly, they experience pleasure in the act of reading and the comfort that comes from rereading a favorite book. Priceless.

MUCH MORE THAN MEMORIZED: READING FAMILIAR BOOKS REQUIRES STRATEGY USE

When children read familiar books on their own, they employ a variety of meaning-making strategies. As Alex reads *Chicka Chicka Boom Boom*, we notice how he uses the illustrations as stepping-stones to help him move through the text. Although he knows the book well because it's been read to him over and over, he still has to pace his reading so that it's synchronized with the illustrations as they appear.

Alex also uses the picture cues to support his comprehension. When he gets stumped, Alex understands that he can rely on the illustrations to help. When his reading goes awry, he also knows he can back up, use the illustrations to reboot, and then start over. Not only is Alex using meaning-making strategies to match the story to the pages, he's also showing signs of resilient problem-solving.

Alex also adds his own meaning-based embellishments to his reading of *Chicka Chicka Book Boom*, such as vocal intonations and reactions that match the tone and drama. He's not relying solely on memory nor is he doing the equivalent of "reading it with his eyes closed." Alex integrates his own interpretations as he reads. He's giving thought to what's going on in different parts of the book based both on the illustrations and his schema from having heard it read aloud before.

What Did Alex Do or Say?	What Might This Suggest or Show?
Alex chooses to read from the familiar pile and selects *Chicka Chicka Boom Boom*.	• Prefers familiar books • Has enthusiasm for familiar books—he made a quick decision about what to read
Alex doesn't hesitate nor does he appeal to Matt when Matt asks him to read *Chicka Chicka Boom Boom*.	• Has a level of confidence with the task • Has schema for reading familiar books
Alex looks at the details in the picture to help him get started with the beginning of the book.	• Realizes the pictures can prompt the story • Uses pictures to help him when something is tricky
Alex reads with a rhyming cadence.	• Remembers that the book rhymes • Understands that rhyming books have a particular "sound" • Reads with a rhyming fluency
Alex doesn't read the text as it's written: *Text reads:* A told B and B told C, "I'll meet you at the top of the coconut tree." "Whee" said D to E F G, "I'll beat you to the top of the coconut tree." Chicka chicka boom boom! Will there be enough room? *Alex reads:* "Here comes A up the coconut tree and B and C, I'll beat you to the top of the coconut tree." D said "whee" to E F G, I'll beat you to the top of the coconut tree."	• Recalls the language of the text and uses it interchangeably throughout the story • Uses the language of the text to anchor him to a page • Uses memory of story but doesn't read based on memorization • Innovates as he reads the text; however, relies on words and syntax that he remembers • Uses pictures to support his reading
Alex begins to turn page, but he ends up staying on the page to continue to read. (1:11)	• Paces his reading to match the illustrations • Navigates meaning between his schema of text and the illustration • Understands that it makes sense when the words match the pictures on the page

Figure 2.2

So even though Alex may know the text well, he's not simply reciting it from memory. He's using what the book offers (illustrations, in this case) to calibrate his reading, he's problem-solving when he encounters glitches, and he's incorporating his own interpretations and vocal stylings.

LANGUAGE BENEFITS

Reading aloud to children regularly and frequently builds their receptive vocabulary and increases their understanding of literary syntax within the helpful and meaningful context of text and illustrations (Christ and Wang 2010). Reading aloud to children provides opportunities to learn new vocabulary, expressions, and concepts, as well as literary language patterns and syntax. When we reread books to them, children move from having been exposed to more vocabulary, language patterns, and syntax to actually taking ownership of more vocabulary, language patterns, and syntax. When children listen to books over and over again and then have the chance to read them on their own, they use the words and syntax of the text themselves. As a bonus, they transfer the literary language, expressions, and vocabulary of the texts into their own oral and written language.

For children who are English language learners, providing plentiful opportunities to hear texts over and over again in the target language is very supportive of language acquisition. They, too, become more comfortable with words, phrases, and syntax, with regard to both comprehension and articulation of the target language. When they have heard language-rich books multiple times, their receptive language abilities become more fine-tuned and discerning. We've noticed, over and over again, that children who are acquiring a new language are willing to express themselves in the target language when they have the security that comes from reading and talking about texts they know well.

All children develop more certainty and confidence about words, phrases, and concepts contained in texts they know well. That confidence increases the likelihood that they'll use the language of the text outside of the reading event. For example, Kathy remembers overhearing her three-year-old son Owen exclaim to his grandma, "Look, Grandma, there's a dirigible!" Kathy and Ian, her husband, hadn't registered him for Tummy Time Vocabulary Development classes when he was a baby. Instead, they simply fulfilled his constant requests to read his beloved Richard Scarry books aloud to him at naptime and at bedtime for weeks, lingering on the page with the dirigible, only because that page was of particular interest for Owen. He independently added the word *dirigible* to his collection of words he knew, and due to the repeated experiences with the word in context, Owen was confident and willing to transfer the acquired vocabulary off of the page and into his life.

Likewise, Matt recalls that when his twins Molly and Natalie were three years old, they used to tell each other that they looked very distinguished. They used this word in logical contexts—when one of them was wearing a dress or a new outfit—so they had a good idea of what the term meant. Matt and his wife, Bridget, were curious about where they had learned the word because it wasn't a word they or their two older children commonly used around the house. One early evening, the girls were rewatching a Barbie video, and much to Matt's surprise (or chagrin), he realized that they got the word from Barbie! Who knew?!

Children are resourceful. This kind of language acquisition and transfer happens all the time, especially when the conditions of repeated exposure to texts (whether they are children's books or children's videos) and opportunities for independent exploration of those familiar texts are regular parts of children's lives.

PLEASURE, COMFORT, CONFIDENCE, AND THE INVITATION OF THE FAMILIAR

During the summer season, lots of musicians tour and perform in huge stadium shows, weekend festivals, or smaller outdoor venues. When the performers have been around for a while, there are some things that are easy to predict. Long-time fans will gather in vintage concert T-shirts hoping that their absolute favorite songs will be on the set list. Throughout the show, the band will sprinkle their old hits among their lesser known or newer music. It's also predictable that when they sing new or unfamiliar songs, the audience will get quieter. The fans can't sing along easily, so they may use that song to go get food or to use the restroom. In contrast (but just as predictable), when the band sings their most familiar songs, the energy of the crowd will rise—vigorous applause will greet the opening measures of the music. Everyone sings and dances, and the audience goes wild. People will be joyful and satisfied, largely because they got what they had hoped for and expected.

When young kids look through a pile of books, there are similar energy patterns when they encounter books they know well. Children open these familiar books and immediately feel at home. The familiar books invite them to "sing along" because children know how they go. Children's high level of comfort with familiar texts increases their engagement with these texts.

When children find familiar books in their homes or classrooms, they are more likely to invite someone else, such as a classmate, an adult, or even a stuffed animal, to sit beside them as they read. Because they know how the book goes, they've got more confidence to read it in front of someone else, and if they love the book, they often want to enjoy it with someone else.

Choosing Books to Make Familiar

During workshops and conferences, parents and teachers often ask for book lists and recommendations. "What are the must-have books?" they want to know. Although we understand the request and desire for advice on the "right" books to read to children, we're hesitant to provide any sort of must-have books list or to name any particular title as "must read." Both Matt and Kathy each have their personal favorites, but their own lists are always changing based on new releases, rediscoveries of oldies but goodies, and titles we learn about from other educators and caregivers. Book choices for homes and classrooms are dependent on so many factors, from children's ages to their preferences, from the text's cultural relevance to content accessibility. So instead of providing any sort of must-read book lists, we offer suggestions for the characteristics of books that are especially helpful to young readers when they are reading books that are familiar to them.

We begin with a resource we've relied upon over the years—the Emergent Storybook Reading approach, developed by Elizabeth Sulzby and William Teale. In their approach, the teacher selects a picture book to read aloud several times to the class within a short time span. For example, a teacher might choose to read aloud *Three Billy Goats Gruff* four times within a week. Once the children know that book well, the teacher makes multiple copies of it available for circulation in the classroom. Classrooms will often have baskets labeled "Star Books" or "Our Favorites" or "Books We Know" that are filled with the texts the teacher has chosen and read aloud multiple times (Sulzby 1985).

CHARACTERISTICS OF BOOKS THAT WORK WELL FOR EMERGENT STORYBOOK READING

According to Sulzby and Teale, books that work especially well in the Emergent Storybook Reading approach have the following characteristics:

- **memorable but not necessarily memorizable**

  In other words, the events in the text are rather easy to remember, but the text itself is hard to memorize. So, a book like *Brown Bear, Brown Bear* that has such a predictable structure and language pattern on each page wouldn't quite work, according to this criterion. Although *Brown Bear, Brown Bear* is likely to be engaging and memorable for children, it's also likely to be very easy to memorize. On the other hand, a book like *The Carrot Seed* is memorable, but a child might not be able to memorize it quite as easily.

- **repeated language**

  Emergent storybooks contain phrases or language patterns that come up often throughout the text. For example, in *Caps for Sale*, there are several places in the book when the peddler says "Caps. Caps for sale, fifty cents a cap." When there are familiar language patterns sprinkled throughout the text, the young reader can use them almost as monkey bar handles that help them get from one end of the text to the other.

- **dialogue**

  When there's dialogue in a text, the adult reader usually reads those portions in an engaging, expressive way. Those parts are often some of the most memorable for the child. The dialogue between the billy goats and the troll in *Three Billy Goats Gruff* is both engaging and expressive, and it serves to hook the reader and also support the reader, similar to repetitive language.

- **high picture support**

  When the pictures and illustrations are closely aligned with the text, it can help to remind children of the story if they begin to lose track. They can rely upon the pictures to help them make their way through their reading of the text. In the Sulzby Classification Scheme, some children might rely solely on the pictures, whereas others use some language from the story, while others might read the text almost verbatim.

- **pleasurable to read over and over**

  This is a critical aspect for selecting a familiar book. First of all, an adult will have to read it repeatedly, so it's important that the book is enjoyable to read aloud. Also, even if the adult loves it, it's important to watch to make sure the children are engaged and find it enjoyable.

A book like *Three Billy Goats Gruff* has many of these characteristics. The plot has repetitive parts that support children as they work to remember the sequence of the story. The dialogue and the sound effect words are engaging and fun to read.

When we're thinking about books that we want to make familiar to children, we do consider and rely upon the Sulzby characteristics. That said, we also want to acknowledge that many teachers have books in their classrooms that families, not teachers, have made familiar to children. We educators don't have total control over which books are most familiar to the children in our classrooms. Often a child knows a particular text very well, even though his teacher didn't handpick the title nor read it aloud repeatedly.

For this reason, we want to expand upon the Emergent Storybook Reading characteristics of familiar books so that we're more inclusive of any book a child knows well, whether or not they became familiar with it in our classrooms. A book like *Knuffle Bunny* by Mo Willems isn't a classic Emergent Storybook Reading program text the way *Three Billy Goats Gruff* is, but *Knuffle Bunny* does have shades of the Sulzby characteristics. *Knuffle Bunny* has tiny bits of repeated language ("Through the park") and dialogue ("Aggle Flaggle Klabble" Trixie cried) that students can use to help them move through the book. It has a clear sequence of events, an engaging story line, and relatively closely aligned picture support. It's also a book many children love to read over and over.

But *Knuffle Bunny* has some advantages over *Three Billy Goats Gruff*. For one thing, *Knuffle Bunny* is much shorter. This will make it more accessible for some children, especially those who are hesitant or those who might be English language learners. It's also a story that's highly relatable because many children have favorite stuffed animals and have experienced the drama of misplacing them.

We also want to expand our field of familiar books to include books that are not necessarily organized as a storybooks. Essentially, storybooks are about "the time something happened." *The time* Trixie lost her Bunny. *The time* Peter played in the snow (*The Snowy Day*). *The time* the Peddler was trying to sell his caps (*Caps for Sale*). In addition to storybooks, we want to include other familiar texts, such as list books and other non-narrative texts.

After all, the books that attract children and that they want to hear over and over are not always written as stories. For this reason, we want to include texts that aren't stories. For example, *Dogs* by Emily Gravett is organized as a list of things the narrator loves about dogs. The text says, "I love big dogs, and small dogs. Tough dogs, and soft dogs. I love dogs that play and dogs that don't." *Dogs* doesn't have a sequence of events, nor is it a book about *the time* something happened. Rather, it's a list of dog characteristics that the narrator loves, and this is a book that children may know and love. We want to accommodate readers who choose books like this, even though this type of text is not a storybook and therefore not aligned with the Sulzby characteristics.

Given this broader view of familiar picture books, here are some characteristics you might consider when selecting books to make familiar to children.

CHARACTERISTICS OF FAMILIAR PICTURE BOOKS

- books that children love and want to read over and over
- books that have memorable features such as repeated phrases, sound words, bits of dialogue, and so forth.
- books that have a reasonable amount of text and length
- books that have supportive illustrations closely aligned with what the text says
- books that are organized as a story or as lists, and so on.
- books that represent a variety of genre (informational books, concept books, wordless picture books, and so on.)
- books that are about topics of interest to children

Even though we've shared some characteristics of the kinds of books to read aloud repeatedly, the truth is that any book that a child loves and knows well is a familiar book that matters. The titles will vary greatly from child to child, from family to family, and from classroom to classroom. The important thing to remember is that when a child interacts with any familiar book, it's much more than cute, and it is a very big deal. It's a reading moment that's worth acknowledging, observing, supporting, encouraging, and instructing. We'll offer ideas for how to do these things in the next chapter.

CHAPTER 3

Instructional Implications When Children Read Familiar Books

Recently during center time, we watched Jesse paw through a few baskets of books in his preschool classroom's reading nook. He looked impatient as he started over a couple of times, flipping books from the back of the basket to the front. He was determined to find something in particular.

After half a minute or so, and just when we were about to intervene, Jesse found what he was looking for: *If You Give a Mouse a Cookie*, by Laura Numeroff. We waited and watched for a few seconds before sitting beside him. "My grandma gave me this book," Jesse said, unprompted. "I got it at home."

"Oh, so have you read it before?" we asked.

"My mom read it to me, and my grandma did, too," he said. He opened up the book and began to read it with a slightly singsong intonation. He was moving quickly through the book, clearly relying on prior knowledge of how the text goes to propel him from one page to the next.

In the old days, had we sat beside Jesse, we might have just smiled and said, "Nice job!" and moved on to another child or to another task. We might have struggled to find an "in" with Jesse, or the entry point for teaching him something in that situation. After all, Jesse pursued this book with intention, and he was engaged as the turned the pages. He didn't ask for any help nor did he seem to need any attention. He was absolutely fine in this moment, so we would have probably moved right on by. Of course, the truth is that there's always something we can do or say, even when the child's work looks airtight.

Mia sat across from Jesse, on the other side of the reading nook. She was talking as she turned the pages of her book, *Where the Wild Things Are*, by Maurice Sendak. Her teacher had recently read it aloud a few times over several days. The children loved it. Mia jabbed at the pages with her pointer finger and "yelled" at the monsters in the book. She said, "You are mean, go away. You're mean, too. Go away, you."

Mia was mildly engaged but not totally committed to reading this text. After turning a page, she would pause and look up and around to see what was going on with her classmates, or she would focus on pulling apart the Band-Aid on her thumb. A couple of times, she looked as if she were on the verge of getting up to find something else to do. Her ties to this text in that moment were vulnerable. This had the telltale signs of a fragile moment about to vanish, the way a bubble will pop with the slightest contact. In the old days, we might have observed Mia briefly and then moved right along, not wanting to break the tenuous moment. We might have given her a thumbs-up and mouthed the words "Keep going" as we kept on going by. Alternatively, we may have decided to sit beside her and offer to read the book aloud to her in an attempt to hold her attention.

In the old days, we would have left Jesse and Mia to do their own thing with their texts. After all, they were both more or less engaged. That might have been the extent of our expectations as we watched young children interact with books on their own before they were able to read conventionally. These days, after observing so many children interacting with familiar texts in ways similar to Jesse and Mia, we can more easily see patterns of strength and vulnerability and natural instructional opportunities.

When we observe with intentionality—with both the intention to figure out what our children are actually doing and the intention to teach them—we are positioned to nudge them toward new options and skills or to support them as they overcome challenges as readers. In this chapter, we'll share some ideas for what we can say as we sit beside kids like Jesse and Mia as they interact with familiar texts.

Familiarizing Ourselves with Familiar

HOW CHILDREN APPROACH AND READ FAMILIAR BOOKS

We've spent time in many early childhood classrooms observing children as they interact with books, and we've noticed trends, similarities, and challenges in the ways children deal with familiar texts. Typically, these observations went like this: we would sit beside a child and offer a choice from an assortment of picture books. When the child selected a familiar one, we asked a variation of this question: "Will you read this book to me?" There was incredible diversity in the range of responses to this question—some children were enthusiastic and confident, similar to the way Natalie approached the reading of *Knuffle Bunny*, and some children stopped altogether and said, "I can't read" or "I don't know how to read yet." Their levels of independence varied, which we discuss in Chapter 7.

We also studied aspects of children's language—their expansiveness and elaboration or lack thereof, their close-to-the-actual text reading and their completely innovated reading—as they read familiar books. We were able to observe four discrete categories of language use, which we describe below. The categories, or levels, we named were influenced by both our observations of children and by the Sulzby Classification Scheme (SCS) for Emergent Reading of Favorite Storybooks (Sulzby 1985).

The SCS is used to observe students as they interact with familiar books that the teacher has read aloud several times. It names and describes eleven different levels of emergent reading of familiar texts. The first two levels include children who label objects and name the actions in the illustrations as they turn the pages, and the last level, the eleventh, describes children who have moved to reading the text conventionally.

In contrast to the SCS, which is applied to storybooks the teacher has read aloud several times to children, our language levels pertain to children reading anything that's familiar—whether it had been read at home or in school, whether it had been read aloud twice or twenty times to the child, whether it's a list book or a storybook. Although we are informed by and value the detail and incremental changes of the eleven levels of SCS, we name fewer language levels that are broader in scope than the SCS simply because the familiar book reading we observe is much broader in scope.

Our language levels apply to children reading familiar books that may have been read aloud to them at home or in school. Our levels apply to children who select familiar books that may have list structures instead of narrative structures. Our intention is to create a guide that will help teachers name what children are doing and consider ways to support them when they are reading *any* text that's familiar, not just the books the teacher has made familiar.

We want to be very clear that we envision both the Sulzby levels and our levels coexisting in classrooms. We are not suggesting ours as a replacement or improvement. Instead, the language levels we describe are another option for teachers (or parents) when their children are reading *anything* familiar, not only teacher-selected books (see Figure 3.1).

Characteristics of and Criteria for Familiar Books per Sulzby's Emergent Storybook Reading, Kindergarten Literacy Program, and Scheme for Emergent Reading	Characteristics of and Criteria for Familiar Book Reading per Collins and Glover
Children can select familiar books from those that have been read aloud by the teacher and designated as familiar/favorites/star books.	Children choose the familiar book they want to read.
Books become familiar because they are read aloud by the teacher to the whole class at least four times in a short period of time.	Books become familiar because someone has read them to the child before (not necessarily the teacher, and no mandate for how many times).
Familiar books meet certain criteria (i.e., storybooks, picture books, preferably contain a repeated refrain, line, or verse throughout story, detailed illustrations, strong picture/text match).	Books may be storybooks, list books, other non-narrative texts, a variety of genres (i.e., informational text). The only criterion for this familiar book is that someone has read the book to the child.

Figure 3.1

OBSERVING CHILDREN WHEN THEY READ FAMILIAR BOOKS TO DETERMINE LANGUAGE LEVELS

As we attended to the language children used as they read familiar books, we noticed variety in the breadth and a range of sophistication of language choices children made. Even though the books were familiar to the children, some read by calling out random objects on the pages whereas others read the text in a way that sounded like they were decoding the words on the pages. Most all of the variations in the children's language use fell into four broad types or levels, whether children were reading books written as stories or books organized as lists, whether they were reading barely familiar books, very familiar books, or anything in between.

We are hesitant to use the word *levels* to describe these language differences because of what the word encourages us to prioritize as teachers (i.e., "Educational mission: raise the levels!") and because of what that word conveys to children ("Yay, I'm a 4!" or "Boo, I'm only a 1").

The levels we name and describe, first and foremost, detail the significance in what children do as they read familiar books. When we see what children can do, we can determine what might be next and teach other possibilities to add to their reading repertoires. The levels we describe are tools for gathering information about children's understandings rather than tools for labeling them. We use these levels to help us calibrate what we might say as we sit beside a child reading a book they know so well.

Familiar Books Language Level 1

A child at this level may or may not state or even realize that she is familiar with the book although the teacher does know for sure that the child has had prior exposure to it. As the child reads, she'll name the action, name the objects, or make comments on each page with or without an intention toward accuracy. As she turns the pages, she doesn't try to connect one page to the next. It sounds like she's beginning anew with each new page. If you were listening in, it would be challenging to figure out what's actually happening on the pages. (Figure 3.2).

 Clip 3.1 *Colton Reads* I Went Walking *and* Rosie's Walk *(Familiar)*
http://smarturl.it/Clip3.1

Familiar Books Language Level 1

Description	Sample Transcript
• The child may or may not express familiarity with the text. • The child attends to pictures and illustrations and may make editorial comments, unrelated to the story. • The child names and labels objects and actions from page to page. • The child may not connect one page to another. • The child may not rely on prior exposure to the text. • The child may not attempt to read with accuracy based on prior exposure.	Child reading *Knuffle Bunny*: "Daddy." "Baby." "Bunny." "They're walking" "There's a dog."

Figure 3.2

In this video montage, Colton is given the option of several familiar books from which to choose, and he selects *I Went Walking* and *Rosie's Walk*. As he reads *I Went Walking*, Colton names what he sees on the pages, such as a cat and dogs. He turns the page and continues to name them, this time adding a quick editorial comment as he reads, "Whoa. A horsey. A horsey. That is so funny. A cow. A red cow. That is so funny." As he reads another familiar book, *Rosie's Walk*, Colton appears to be studying the pages. He doesn't name objects yet he does react to what he sees by saying, "whoa."

For many young children, the language level for reading familiar books is tied closely to the strengths and vulnerabilities they bring as language users across the day. Whether or not the challenges Colton faced as he reads *Rosie's Walk* and *I Went Walking* are connected to his expressive language skill is certainly important to consider, but what he did as he read these books is quite representative of how reading sounds at Language Level 1 for any children, whether they are native speakers of English, English language learners, or children with expressive language challenges. Of course, as a teacher confers with young readers as they read familiar books, he would observe the language level of their reading while also considering how to support the children's language use across the day.

Familiar Books Language Level 2

When a child is reading a familiar book at Language Level 2, he acknowledges his familiarity. He uses his prior experience with the book to read in a way that's intentionally more accurate contentwise and aligned with how the text goes. He relies heavily on pictures and illustrations and reads it in a way that's relatively true to the actual plot or story line. If you were listening in without looking at the text, you'd be able to get a gist of the story (Figure 3.3).

Clip 3.2 *Dion Reads* Three Billy Goats Gruff *(Familiar)*

http://smarturl.it/Clip3.2

As we watch Dion read *Three Billy Goats Gruff*, we can tell right away that this is a familiar book for him because Dion reads it with content accuracy. For example, he says the goats are looking for food, even though there aren't any picture clues showing that. He's remembering that detail because the story is familiar to him. Also, Dion calls the goats "billy goats." It's unlikely that he would call them that unless he had heard the book before.

Familiar Books Language Level 2

Description of Familiar Books Language Level 2	Sample Transcript
• The child expresses familiarity. • The child attends to pictures and illustrations. • The child names objects and actions with more detail. • The child connects one page to another to create a cohesive reading. • The child relies on prior exposure to the text to read in a way that's more accurate content-wise to the text.	Child reading **Knuffle Bunny**: "I know this one. I have it at home!" / "There's Trixie and her dad going to the laundry-mat." / "They walked in the park / and there's the school / and now they're at the laundry-mat / Look at Trixie. She's playing / There goes her doll. / She put money into the washer / Uh-oh." /

Figure 3.3

It's important to note that the goal for our readers in these language levels isn't content accuracy or text accuracy for accuracy's sake. We wouldn't correct a child and say, "Those are billy goats, not just goats." Instead, we're observing and noting children's level of content accuracy to determine how much language and content a child remembers from prior exposures to the text. That helps us think about ways we can teach them to use those experiences to help them read the book independently and about how we might support acquisition of vocabulary.

Familiar Books Language Level 3

Children at this level express their familiarity with the text and use their schema to read in a way that's even more accurate contentwise. At this level, the language the child uses is also more closely aligned with the actual words in the text. Children still rely on pictures and illustrations to help them move with content accuracy through the text, but now they incorporate more of the actual words and syntax in their reading (Figure 3.4).

 Clip 3.3 *Natasha Reads* Go, Dog. Go! *(Familiar)*
http://smarturl.it/Clip3.3

In this video, Natasha reads *Go, Dog. Go!* in a way that's largely aligned with the content of the book. As she reads, she's using more words and phrases that are directly from the

Familiar Books Language Level 3

Description of Familiar Books Language Level 3	Sample Transcript
• The child expresses high level of familiarity. • The child attends to pictures and illustrations. • The child names objects and actions with more text-based detail and story language. • The child connects one page to another to create a cohesive reading. • The child relies on prior exposure to the text to read in a way that's more accurate content-wise and language-wise to the text.	Child reading **Knuffle Bunny**: "Trixie went with her daddy / They walked and walked and walked down the block / and in the park / the school / and into the Laundromat. / Trixie is helping her daddy."

Figure 3.4

story. For example, on the pages where the dogs are greeting each other, Natasha says, "Do you like my hat?" and then "No, I don't." She could have conveyed this meaning based on the illustrations by using made-up phrases, yet she chose language that nearly matched the actual text. This is one of the most distinguishing characteristics of children who are reading with characteristics of Language Level 3.

We notice that as Natasha uses the pictures rather than the words to guide her reading, she doesn't read with a consistent sense of conventional left-to-right directionality. On one page, she tracks an illustration from right to left; on another page, she tracks from bottom to top. Yet, even so, she's monitoring for meaning in the pictures. On these pages she uses what she remembers about the actions in the story and what she can see in the pictures to make up words and syntax. In other words, Natasha doesn't use the exact language from the book consistently from start to finish, yet she's resourceful when her recall of the actual text breaks down. Although she moves between Language Levels 2 and 3 and can use support with directionality, we'd consider Natasha's reading to be mostly characteristic of a child who is using language within the Level 3 criteria.

Familar Books Language Level 4

Children at this level use their schema from prior exposures, and they rely heavily on pictures and illustrations to read in a way that's very accurate. Even more so than Level 3, children at this level incorporate more words and language from the text in their reading. They read with expression and intonation, imitating the way they've heard the book read aloud before. These children also transfer the language of the book into their real lives (Figure 3.5).

Familiar Books Language Level 4

Description of Familiar Books Language Level 4	Sample Transcript
• The child expresses high level of familiarity. • The child relies on prior exposure to the text in the book to read with accurate meaning. • The child attends to pictures and illustrations. • The child connects one page to another to create a cohesive reading. • The child reads aloud with accuracy, using words, phrases, and syntax of the text. • The child reads with intonation and expression.	Child reading *Knuffle Bunny*: "Not long ago, before she could speak words, Trixie went on a errand with her daddy. / They went down the block / through the park / past the school / and the Laundromat / Trixie helped her daddy put laundry in the machine / She even put the money in the machine."

Figure 3.5

Clip 3.4 *Emily Reads* The Very Hungry Caterpillar *(Familiar)*
http://smarturl.it/Clip3.4

As we watch Emily read *The Very Hungry Caterpillar*, we can tell that not only has she heard the book many times before, she has also had opportunities to read this book several times before. She is immediately comfortable. Her reading for each page is either exactly the same as the actual text or almost the same. She maintains content and language accuracy throughout the text, rather than moving back and forth between levels. In fact, if you were sitting nearby as Emily (or any child at this language level) read this book, you would think that she is using print strategies to read conventionally due to how similar her reading aligns with the actual text.

A CAVEAT, OF COURSE

It's important to note that sometimes children might present characteristics from more than one language level within the reading of one text. For example, we sat beside Ava, a first grader, as she read *Click Clack Moo: Cows That Type*, a book that her teacher had read a few times to her class. Ava began the book tentatively, saying things like, "There are the cows." As she read on, however, she began to integrate more of the language from the text, using words like *strike* and actual text syntax such as "There will be no electric blanket." Within this one text, Ava was moving from one level to another.

Children also move among the levels from one book to another. We observed Devon and noted how his language levels varied from book to book. For example, he sounded like a junior teacher as he read *How Do Dinosaurs Say Good Night?* by Jane Yolen, whereas he largely improvised his way through other texts that his teacher said he knew well.

Devon and Ava and so many other children provide further evidence that these Language Levels aren't fixed, linear, or necessarily chronological reading-development milestones. We would never say that a child is "Language Level 3" because his reading may vary within a text and certainly across texts. Instead, we might observe that Sophia reads *Knuffle Bunny* with characteristics of Language Level 2, and then we'd use that knowledge to helps us think about ways we can support her. As she proceeds through the book, we could teach Sophia to use what she knows of the story to talk like Trixie. We might nudge her toward some of the Level 3 characteristics, especially reading with the language of the text in mind.

Clip 3.5 *Jazzalynn Reads* Clip-Clop *(Unfamiliar)*

http://smarturl.it/Clip3.25

We invite you to watch Jazzalyn read *Clip-Clop* for the first time. Even though this is an unfamiliar text, it shows how children's language levels can change within one book. It begins with Matt showing her how she could read this book, and she reads it by labeling the animals she sees and telling where they are. Later, however, her language use and meaning making seem to surge. Rather than simply saying that the animals are on the horse, she infers that they are about to fall off. She even justifies her inference by pointing out that the cat is holding on tight to the horse's neck. Her language and her meaning making have become more sophisticated in a short amount of time. For Jazzalyn and most other children, it is likely that they will move back and forth between language levels, whether the books are familiar or unfamiliar.

Conferring to Support Students Within and to Nudge Students Across Levels

Lucy Calkins' groundbreaking conferring triad "Research—Decide—Teach" (Calkins 1994) continues to be a powerful mantra for teachers to bear in mind as they confer—whether we're conferring with young readers, writers, artists, mathematicians, scientists, playground rivals, heartbroken friends, and so on. Still, even if we have an effective conferring architecture, it's important to realize that conferring is informed improvisation. Although it's true that we can anticipate conferring possibilities because we carry schema and prior experiences with our children as well as in-the-moment observations, it's not easy, nor very advisable, to tightly plan or script out a conference before it happens. In other words, even if we approach Luca with a certainty that he reads mostly at Language Level 3, we don't advise entering a conference as if your sole teaching duty is to move him from Level 3 to Level 4. He might need some support with other aspects of his reading that may be more urgent.

We can't know exactly what we'll want to say to a child, even if we know ahead of time what language level she tends to operate within. Each child demands from us an individualized and differentiated approach with regard to the reading instruction we offer and the personal connection we make.

As we work with young children just beginning to read texts independently yet not conventionally, we always keep in mind that a conference is not a formal assessment opportunity or an assigned performance task. We're not trying to make the child jump through hoops. Our inclination when we work with young readers is always to go and meet the child where she is rather than trying to coax her or pull her over to where want her to be. We watch what she does for a bit, and then, in a conversational tone, we help her make more meaning, engage more intentionally with the text, or talk about her thinking as she reads.

STARTING A CONFERENCE

We want to see what the child does in the name of reading books, so we might be inclined to ask the child, "Can you read this to me?" For some children, that question poses no problem or risk. The child will gladly do his version of reading as he's grateful to have an audience. Other children might shrink away from this request and say they can't read.

We've found that it often works to sidle our way into a conference. We might open with a question like, "May I listen to you read this?" This approach is different than "Can you read this to me?" by only a few words, but children tend to respond more comfortably when we ask if we can listen to them read rather than asking them if they can read. Beginning a conference with "May I listen to you read this?" presumes the child is reading, and it doesn't suggest to the child that she has to do anything different. Children are more likely to continue on, doing what they can do, whereas asking, "Can you read this to me?" might sound like we're requesting a performance or putting children on the spot. It also might imply that we're not sure if the child can read the book. Instead, we want to communicate that we know she can.

We pay close attention to what children say and do for a few pages before we jump in to confer. As we watch and listen, we get an idea about what they know already about reading and making meaning in general and what they know about the book specifically. We use this information to decide if it makes more sense to teach the children to do something new as readers or to support and strengthen what they're doing at that point, especially if it seems nascent or unsteady. We also make a point to jot notes about our observations and the instruction we offered during our conferences. We've included sample note-taking sheets for conferences in Appendix A (see pp. 167–168).

Each child demands from us an individualized and differentiated approach with regard to the reading instruction we offer and the personal connection we make.

CONFERRING: FAMILIAR BOOKS LANGUAGE LEVEL 1

When we're working with children who read familiar texts in a way that is mostly aligned with Familiar Books Language Level 1 characteristics, our big intention is to teach toward elaboration using picture clues and schema. We coax and invite the child to use more language to read the book and we also teach some strategies that readers can use to help them remember the story (Figure 3.6).

CONFERRING: FAMILIAR BOOKS LANGUAGE LEVEL 2

When young readers have moved beyond the one- and two-word labeling of texts as they read toward more elaboration, we can support their use of strategies to maintain cohesiveness in their reading (Figure 3.7). We can help them read the text with more content accuracy, teaching them to recall what they know about the book or the topic, and to use their familiarity to their advantage. We'll also add some fix-it strategies for when they encounter difficulties, such as how to regain their footing when they lose their place in the text or when they forget what they know about it.

CONFERRING: FAMILIAR BOOKS LANGUAGE LEVEL 3

In Familiar Books Language Level 3, children's reading is closely aligned with what's happening on the pages. They strive to remember how the text goes, and their reading holds content accuracy. They also express more vocabulary and phrasing that matches the text itself. They use characters' names consistently, or if the book is informational, they'll include more specific domain vocabulary. The child uses more literary syntax rather than simply relying on her own oral language patterns to represent the text (Figure 3.8), and the transitions between pages are smoother.

Familiar Books Language Level 1

Examples of What a Child Might Do While Reading	What Might We Do or Say to Support or Nudge This Child?	Example of an Interaction Between Child and Adult (Knuffle Bunny by Mo Willems)
Names and labels characters and/or objects	• We can ask what the characters/objects are doing to help the child move from one- or two-word labeling to sentences and toward more elaboration. • We can model full sentences and elaboration.	Child: "A girl and a Daddy." Adult: "Yeah, there's Trixie and her daddy. Let's think about and say what they're doing together." Child: "Walking?" Adult: "Trixie and her daddy are walking down the street."
Calls out details on the page that may or may not be vital to the story	• We can help to refocus the child toward the main action on the page or we can support the child in elaborating. • We can model how to connect the details with the main action of the page.	Child: "There's a doggie!" Adult: "I see that dog, too. He's a little one, isn't he? He's doing something. Let's say what he's doing."
Attends to pictures and illustrations, and makes editorial comments about them that may be unrelated to the story	• We can help the child connect his thinking to the story or we can support the child toward elaborating on his ideas and thinking. • We can model how to bring random ideas back to the text.	Child: "This looks funny." Adult: "What is funny?" Child: (points to Trixie's teeth) Adult: "What about her teeth?" Child: (points to spaces between her teeth) Adult: "Oh, I see what you mean. She's got baby teeth! With spaces between them! Trixie is a little girl with little teeth. That makes sense!" Child: "Trixie is a little like my baby sister!"
May not connect or carry the text through from one page to another	• We can help the child carry character or story line or concept from one page to the next. • We can model how to carry one page to the next to create cohesion between pages by using connecting words such as, "And then . . ." and "After that . . ."	Adult: "Oh, look. There's Trixie and her daddy again. What are they doing now?" Child: "Walking." Adult: "Trixie and her daddy are walking down the street . . ." (turns page). Child: "Park." Adult: "And then Trixie and her daddy walk through the park" (turns page).

Figure 3.6

Familiar Books Language Level 1 (Continued)

Examples of What a Child Might Do While Reading	What Might We Do or Say to Support or Nudge This Child?	Example of an Interaction Between Child and Adult (Knuffle Bunny by Mo Willems)
Reads passively or perhaps in a disengaged way, using one-word labels and naming actions	• We can ask questions to help the child invest more in the book. We can ask the child to think about why things happened and what characters might be thinking or feeling. • We can show the child how to act out the story and how to give voice to characters. • We can model how to "get into" the story.	Child: "The girl and her daddy are walking (turns page). They're walking (turns page). Walking." Adult: "Look at Trixie and her daddy walking through the park. Maybe he's saying, 'Wait for me, Trixie.' What might Trixie say to her daddy?" Child: "Running!" Adult: "Hey, Trixie, slow down! You're so fast!"

Figure 3.6 (Continued)

Familiar Books Language Level 2

Examples of What a Child Might Do While Reading	What Might We Do or Say to Support or Nudge This Child?	Example of an Interaction Between Child and Adult (Knuffle Bunny by Mo Willems)
Expresses familiarity and attends to pictures and illustrations	• We can remind the child to use what she knows as she reads the text. • We can teach the child how to use the pictures/illustrations to remind her of the text if she forgets or loses her place or to help her add language from the text.	Child: "Hey, I know this book. I have it at home and my mom reads it to me." Adult: "Oh, that's so helpful to know the book. You can remember how it goes to help you read it." Child: "Trixie and her daddy went for a walk." Adult: (fingers walking on the page) "Down the block . . ." Child: "Through the park and this school. And they got to the, I forgot what it's called." Adult: "Look at the picture. They're doing laundry in it . . ." Child: "The laundry-mat. In the laundry-mat."

Figure 3.7

Familiar Books Language Level 2 (Continued)

Examples of What a Child Might Do While Reading	What Might We Do or Say to Support or Nudge This Child?	Example of an Interaction Between Child and Adult (Knuffle Bunny **by Mo Willems**)
Names objects and actions with more detail	• We can begin to remind him of the language of the text by saying, "What did the character say?" or "Oh, that's called a _____. Remember?" • We can support her to infer what's going on in the text.	Child: "Trixie said 'apple apple aggle flaggle' or something like that because her bunny is lost." Adult: "Yeah, look at her face! She looks like this (makes face). How do you think she's feeling right now?" Child: "She's sad." Adult: "What makes you think Trixie is sad?" Child: "She lost her bunny and she loves her bunny." Adult: "That is really sad."
Connects one page to another to create a cohesive reading	• We can support the child by modeling the language that connects pages. • We can show him how he can turn back a page to remind himself of what's going on, in case he gets stumped.	Child: "Trixie said, 'apple apple flaggle.' She's sad." (turns page and looks at it; skips past the page where the dad says that they're going home) Adult: (turns back page to "aggle flaggle klabble" page) "Trixie realized something, and she said 'aggle flaggle klabble.' She was sad (turns the page) but her dad said . . ." Child: "And the Daddy said, 'Let's go home' because he didn't understand her words."
Relies on prior exposure to the text to read with content accuracy	• We can begin to support the child with more language-based accuracy, reminding the child of words from the text itself. • When the child reads with attention to accuracy to the plot and meaning of the text, we can support inferential thinking by pausing to talk about what's happening on particular pages.	Child: "Then they left, and Trixie knew she forgot." Adult: "A block or so later, Trixie realized something, didn't she?" Child: "She realized something, that she forgot her bunny."

Figure 3.7 (Continued)

Familiar Books Language Level 3

Examples of What a Child Might Do While Reading	What Might We Do or Say to Support or Nudge This Child?	Example of an Interaction Between Child and Adult (Knuffle Bunny by Mo Willems)
Continues building on the skills of Familiar Books Language Levels 1 and 2 Expresses high level of familiarity Attends to pictures and illustrations Names objects and actions with more text-based detail and story language Connects one page to another to create a cohesive reading	• We can continue to support the child in elaborating more and sharing her thinking about the texts. • We can support the child in reading with more expression and prosody because he knows the story so well. • We can continue to model full sentences and elaboration as well as cohesive reading across pages.	Child: "Later Trixie turned to daddy and said, 'apple flapple klabble.'" Adult: "Look how upset she is ... let's try to sound like Trixie! How would she say it?" Child: (with worried voice and facial expression) "Apple Flapple Klabble?" Adult: "Ooh, you looked and sounded so worried and sad. Let's read it like that, okay? Let's sound sad and worried" (turns back to the page to where this occurs) Child: (with a sad, worried voice) "Later Trixie said to Daddy, 'APPLE FLAPPLE KLABBLE!'"
Relies on prior exposure to the text to read in a way that's more accurate content-wise and language-wise to what the text actually says	• We can let the child know that she sounded just like an author when she read. • We can remind the child of the text-based words/phrases so he can integrate them into his reading. • We can support the child with oral language acquisition by checking to make sure she understands words and phrases she is using.	

Figure 3.8

CONFERRING: FAMILIAR BOOKS LANGUAGE LEVEL 4

There is a small and nuanced difference between characteristics of readers at Familiar Books Language Level 3 and Familiar Books Language Level 4. In Level 4, children read the text in a way that is largely accurate, both with regard to language and content, and they also read with fluency and expression. The child's transitions between pages are smooth, and, similar to the highest Sulzby levels, if you were to close your eyes, you might think the child is reading conventionally. Additionally, at this level, a child might begin to recognize and read some of the words of the text conventionally, or at the very least, he might be interested in locating words on the page (Figure 3.9).

CONFERRING WITH YOUNG READERS IN FAMILIAR PICTURE BOOKS: AN EXAMPLE

Mary Alice Berry, our friend and a wonderful teacher, kindly videotaped conferences she had with young readers who were reading familiar books before they could read conventionally. We invite you to watch and notice how Mary Alice affirms and supports what the children are doing while also trying to nudge them toward growth and new approaches.

Clip 3.6 *Hannah Reads* Bad Case of Stripes *(Familiar)*
http://smarturl.it/Clip3.6

In this conference, Mary Alice shows Hannah something she can add to her reading repertoire. Instead of simply listening to Hannah read this text or just noting her language level, Mary Alice uses in-conference research to help her decide what to teach in that moment. Hannah begins by talking about the pages as if she's describing them and not reading them (i.e., "Here I think she doesn't know what to wear"), which suggests that although Hannah knows this book, she may not know it very well. It may also suggest that Hannah isn't quite sure how to begin a book in a literary way. To help Hannah shift from narrating the pictures to putting them together into a more cohesive text that sounds more storylike (because in this case the familiar text features a story), Mary Alice nudges her to attend to the characters and use the action in the pictures to think about what the characters might say. The combination of Hannah's schema of the text (however slight it may be at this point) and her inventive dialogue will help her sound like she's reading rather than simply describing what's on each page. This is something that she can do across pages to help her

Familiar Books Language Level 4

Examples of What a Child Might Do While Reading	What Might We Do or Say to Support or Nudge This Child?	Example of an Interaction Between Child and Adult (Knuffle Bunny by Mo Willems)
Continues to build on the skills of Familiar Book Levels 1, 2, and 3 Reads in an accurate and fluent way, perhaps missing a word here or there Expresses high level of familiarity Attends to pictures and illustrations Names objects and actions with more text-based detail and story language Connects one page to another to create a cohesive reading Reads with content accuracy and language accuracy	• We can continue to support the child in elaborating more and sharing her thinking about the texts. • We can support the child in reading with more expression and prosody because he knows the story so well. • We can continue to model full sentences and elaboration as well as cohesive reading across pages.	Child: (pauses as he reads and points under a word) "Does that say 'Trixie'?" Adult: "What makes you ask?" Child: "I saw it on this page, too" (goes back a couple of pages). Adult: "What makes you think it says 'Trixie'?" Child: "It's the part with Trixie and it's like Trey's name here with the T." Adult: "Well, huh. You are right. It does say 'Trixie.' You can read it like this" (shows the child how to point under the words in that part).
Reads the text with accuracy with regard to content, language, and literary syntax Reads with intonation and expression that matches the tone of the text May read with attention to print or may attempt to read the text conventionally	• We can let the child know that she sounded just like a storyteller when she read. • We can check for understanding in natural and supportive ways. • We can support the child with oral language acquisition by checking to make sure he understands words and phrases he is using. • We can ask the child to point to some words as she reads.	Child: "Long ago, before she could say words, Trixie went on a errand with her daddy. / They went down the block / through the park / past the school / and in the laundry-mat / Trixie helped her daddy put laundry in the machine / She even could put the money in the machine. / Then they left." Adult: "Wow, you sound just like a grown-up reading this." Child: "A block later, Trixie said, 'Aggle Flaggle Klaggle!'" Adult: "Ooh, what's happening here?" Child: "Trixie left her Knuffle Bunny in the laundry-mat and she's trying to tell daddy." Adult: "But he says let's go home." Child: "Yeah, he doesn't understand because she's talking in baby talk."

Figure 3.9

make it sound like a book. Mary Alice first shows her how this strategy works, and then she extends an invitation for Hannah to try it on another page.

Although we've categorized the ways that children may approach the reading of familiar texts into language levels and offered ideas for what to say to children to nudge them forward, we want to be clear that our biggest priority in these conferences with early readers is to make connections with them and to enjoy the book together. It's important to bear in mind that we aren't just teaching children how to read, we're also supporting them so they love to read.

CHAPTER 4

Reading Unfamiliar Books

ecently Matt watched the Alfred Hitchcock classic *Rear Window* with his eleven-year-old daughters, Molly and Natalie. Matt had watched the film many times, but this was Molly and Natalie's first time. They all enjoyed the movie and had lots to talk about afterward. Even so, Molly and Natalie's experience of watching *Rear Window* was quite different from Matt's, largely because the thinking work required to make meaning when watching something for the first time is quite different from when one is watching something familiar.

Molly and Natalie had to pay very close attention to what was going on in the film as they searched for clues to help them understand the story. They had to closely follow both the big action and plot moves while also attending to small and subtle details. Meanwhile, because of his familiarity, Matt had the luxury to choose where to focus his attention.

As they watched the film, Molly and Natalie scrambled to create, revise, or reject theories about characters and predictions for outcomes. They inferred reasons why Thorwald behaved the way he did, and they had to figure out whether or not the motivations for his actions were truly malevolent. They made predictions about what was going to happen, and they had to revise their predictions on the run as more story information was revealed. Molly and Natalie experienced a higher level of tension than Matt, simply because they had no certainty about how things would turn out. They worried when Grace Kelly's character climbed into Thorwald's window. They felt a deep sense of sweet relief with the resolution at the end.

Because Matt knew the story and the outcome, he didn't need to make and revise any predictions. He didn't worry about the characters in the same way that Natalie and Molly did, and although he still felt tension and suspense as he rewatched this classic, he wasn't on the same emotional roller coaster as Molly and Natalie.

Matt's familiarity with the film enabled him to use his cognitive energies in different ways. Because he wasn't trying to figure everything out, Matt noticed things he missed in previous viewings. He experienced a "closer watch" of the movie and a deeper understanding of the relationships among the characters. He attended to the dialogue because he didn't need to catch every detail and nuance of the plot, and instead of simply feeling the tension, Matt was trying to figure out the moves and techniques Hitchcock used to create such tension and suspense. His experience was also more social and extroverted because he could divide his attention between the film and his daughters. Matt watched his daughters watch the film, and he enjoyed their reactions and questions as much as he enjoyed the film.

The different types and depths of meaning making experienced by Matt and his daughters weren't qualitatively better or worse or more or less important than one another's. All three were engaged and focused, and they finished the film having things to say about it. But even though they watched and enjoyed the same film, their experiences were fundamentally different.

... find ways to entice children to read unfamiliar books and to then support them so that they are doing so with engagement, intention, and meaning-making priorities.

Although this anecdote describes viewers engaged in both first-time watching and rewatching a film, it can easily be generalized to an experience of young children engaged with a book. Imagine if Mem Fox's classic picture book *Koala Lou* replaced Alfred Hitchcock's classic film *Rear Window* in the anecdote above. Imagine if Molly and Natalie were looking through the pages of *Koala Lou* for the first time whereas Matt was reading it for the tenth time. Although we can imagine the three of them enjoying the story, the cognitive demands of reading something for the first time are quite different from reading something again and again and again. It is in the best interest of our young readers to provide them with lots of experiences with both kinds of reading.

In this chapter, we suggest that providing opportunities for children to read unfamiliar texts before they're reading conventionally is empowering and engaging. The thinking work it requires, the resourcefulness it calls for, and the challenges it presents make it worth our while to find ways to entice children to read unfamiliar books and to then support them so that they are doing so with engagement, intention, and meaning-making priorities. These experiences with unfamiliar books are important to children's development as readers, meaning-makers, risk-takers, and problem-solvers.

Although most young children have some experience rereading well-loved, favorite books, either at home or in school, it is less common for them to independently pick out and stick with a book that is unknown or unfamiliar. We've watched children in pre-K classrooms rummage through a basket containing familiar and unfamiliar books. Most often, the children flip right past texts they've never seen before to get to *Brown Bear, Brown Bear, What Do You See?* or the well-loved version of *The Three Little Pigs* with the taped-up pages.

We begin with the premise that reading unfamiliar books at home or at school activates a very different kind of thinking on the part of the child. When kids pick up a book they've never seen or heard before, they don't have any prior experience with that text to rely upon. They can't recall (or, therefore, mimic) their mother's voice when she reads a particular page. They don't have their dad's explanation of what's happening in a certain part and so they can't then use that prior knowledge to anchor them to the text. They don't have an experience of listening to their teacher read it aloud to them. They don't have the security of knowing a repeated refrain that helps them hold on to the story across pages.

> *When children actively choose to read unknown texts and feel empowered to do so, their image of themselves as readers and their vision of reading are expanded.*

When a child reads an unknown book for the first time, she is called upon to imagine and invent what is happening on each page. It requires a deeper level of attention to illustrations and details within and across pages. It requires self-reliant inferring in which she integrates the information on the page and across pages with her own experiences and knowledge. It requires the child to call upon her language stores.

When children actively choose to read unknown texts and feel empowered to do so, their image of themselves as readers and their vision of reading are expanded. They become more confident, more willing, and more able to interact with any text, regardless of whether it is known or unknown.

As we consider the work that children do as they read unfamiliar texts, we have to keep in mind that the act of reading is made up of much more than just decoding the words on the page even though so much of the instructional focus and adult concern for our youngest readers is about getting them to decode. Although this is certainly an obvious and important part of becoming a well-rounded reader, a narrowly centered focus on teaching young children to decode at the expense of other kinds of experiences with texts may actually strip away their very early sense of agency (Johnston 2004) and comfort with books.

However, if we expand our own view of early reading to include all the work children do before they're reading conventionally, we see so much more than a young child not yet reading the words on a page. We see intention and purpose. We see problem-solving and resourcefulness. We see meaning making and the development of a healthy reading identity. With this expansive view of what it means to be a reader, we are more likely to observe, value, support, and extend what children do as readers before they start to decode words.

Still, we want to be clear: we're not deemphasizing the importance of teaching children to be skillful word-solvers and proficient decoders, nor are we suggesting that we withhold that instruction if a child is clearly ready and waiting for it. Instead we are suggesting that it's also worth prioritizing young children's comprehension, meaning making, and thinking work in all kinds of texts, including unfamiliar books. Providing young children with lots of opportunities and encouragement to read unfamiliar books, in addition to the ones they know so well and love so much, helps them to become adventurous, confident readers who are highly engaged meaning-makers.

As an example of a child reading an unfamiliar text, we've included a short video of Wade reading *Zoom,* a picture book by Diane Adams and illustrated by Kevin Luthardt. Wade is four and attends preschool. He chose to read this book, although nobody has ever read it to him before, nor has he ever looked through it prior to the moment on video.

Please take a moment to watch the video and gather your thoughts before reading ahead to our analysis. Here are some questions you might consider as you watch:

1. What might Wade's words and actions reveal about his ideas of what it means to read?

2. What does Wade do and say as he reads to help him make meaning?

3. What do you notice about Wade's affect and engagement throughout the reading session?

Clip 4.1 *Wade Reads* Zoom! *(Unfamiliar)*
http://smarturl.it/Clip4.1

Anyone who watches Wade finds different points of interest, and each time we view it, we see something new and thought-provoking. Figure 4.1 is a small collection of things we've noticed, so far.

What Did Wade Do or Say?	What Does This Suggest or Show?
Started reading the text without any adult support or encouragement.	• Confidence • Comfort with texts, a willingness to read independently • Willingness to take risks with unknown content
Read through the whole text with momentum and engagement.	• Stamina for meaning making and for finishing a text • Enjoyment in books
Read: "The roller coaster ride, he had some tickets for the dinosaur roller coaster."	• Attention to major and minor details in the illustrations • Effective integration of the details to make a story
Read: "Pull the lever."	• Creation of dialogue for the characters based on what the illustration and his schema suggested • Use of domain-specific vocabulary (lever) • Activation of schema for roller coasters and amusement park rides
Read: "They went on and on and on, past lots and lots of dinosaur parts and even more."	• Use of literary language and syntax • Carrying the story across pages by connecting the illustrations from one page to another
Read: "The dad was getting scared. It was getting worse with the dad."	• Inferring characters' feelings by looking closely at facial expressions • Inferring characters' feelings by activating schema
Read: "Then they go (gestures). They go zig and zag and then a backwards flip. Then under the ocean. There's lots of bad types of dinosaurs."	• Reading with expression and intonation • Use of gestures to act out part of the story • Use of descriptive words for roller coaster's movement
Read: "Then inside of a tunnel. That was fun."	• Addition of his own personal response as an aside to the story
Read: "And the ride is over. And then ... (he turns the page, and then turns back a page) and then he wants to go back. He goes all by hisself."	• Use of resources in the text (illustration) to confirm/revise understanding
Read: "His dad hated it." "He's too old."	• Conclusions about characters accounting for the action within and at the end of the story • Inferring character's feelings and attitudes
When Matt talks to Wade, he looks up off the text but not at Matt, and he responds with what sounds like a slightly exasperated tone.	• Reluctance to interrupt his reading to respond to questions

Figure 4.1

It's important to remember that Wade had not seen this book before. Despite this, many of his inferences turn out to be aligned with what's actually going on in the story. Wade relies heavily on clues in the illustrations, attending to both the major and minor details in the pictures to help him form a sequential, comprehensible story.

These few minutes of Wade reading an unfamiliar book reveal so much about what Wade believes it means to be a reader and what he understands about reading. It suggests a high level of comfort with picture books and a strategic stance toward figuring out what's going on in a story. Wade is proactive and engaged with a text he has never seen before, and this stance will serve him well as he inevitably encounters many other unfamiliar texts.

As early childhood teachers and parents of young children consider what texts to make available for the children in their care, we advocate that classrooms and bedrooms, bookshelves and nightstands be piled high with all kinds of books, including many unfamiliar books.

Advantages of Reading Unfamiliar Books

There are many benefits for children when they have opportunities to reread familiar, well-loved books, as we described in Chapter 2. In this chapter, we share several important advantages for our youngest readers when they have opportunities to read and encouragement to negotiate meaning in unfamiliar books as well.

We consider a book to be unfamiliar when it meets one of the following conditions:

1. The child has never seen it before and is looking through it for the first time.
2. The child may have looked through the text once or twice, but the text has never been read aloud to her.

Wherever young children search for books, whether they're looking in library shelves, bookstore displays, yard sale bins, or websites, the vast majority of texts they'll encounter will be unfamiliar to them. For this reason, it's important to help children feel comfortable and empowered to read these texts, even though they may not have had the good fortune of hearing it read aloud before. When children have regular opportunities to read unknown books before they're able to read conventionally, they do some important tasks as readers and they develop some constructive learning habits. The act of reading unfamiliar texts demands that young children:

- construct meaning and innovate using a variety of sources of information and essential reading strategies
- problem-solve independently and take managed risks as they explore a safe unknown
- develop stamina to stay with a challenging task and hone their abilities to stay focused.

When children read an unfamiliar book, they are required to innovate, bringing more of their own schema, personality, and purpose to the task. We invite you to view this video clip, in which you'll see Sha'Nya read *Hello Twins* for the first time.

Clip 4.2 *Sha'Nya Reads* Hello Twins *(Unfamiliar)*
http://smarturl.it/Clip4.2

Sha'Nya gets to the page where one of the twins, Charlotte, is building a block tower while Simon, her brother, lies belly down on the floor with his arm and pointer finger extended toward the base of Charlotte's tower. Sha'Nya reads this illustration, "Simon's knocking it over." Matt tells her that another child, Garrett, looked at the same page and thought that Simon was helping to hold up the tower.

Clip 4.3 *Garrett Reads* Hello Twins *(Unfamiliar)*
http://smarturl.it/Clip4.3

Even though the text actually says that that Simon likes to knock down block towers, and Sha'Nya's reading of that page was aligned with the actual text, Garrett's interpretation does work as he inferred the meaning from the picture and from his own experiences.

If we were to ask Garrett what made him think that Simon is trying to hold up the tower, he might say that Simon is helping his sister or that he likes blocks or he might simply say that Simon is holding up the tower because he's putting his finger near it. If we asked Sha'Nya what makes her think Simon is trying to knock down the tower, she may say that Simon is pushing it with his finger. In both cases, Garrett and Sha'Nya's responses are possible when they draw upon both on their schema for that sort of situation and the information that the illustration offers.

If we had read aloud *Hello Twins* to Sha'Nya and Garrett first, their alternative interpretations would vanish. They would know what the author and illustrator intended and they would understandably hold tight to that "official" meaning.

Because this is an unfamiliar text to both Sha'Nya and Garrett, we're giving them opportunities to make hypotheses, inferences, and predictions using the clues the book provides along with all of the experiences and schema they bring to their reading.

CHILDREN CONSTRUCT MEANING AND INNOVATE USING A VARIETY OF SOURCES OF INFORMATION AND ESSENTIAL READING STRATEGIES.

When children read familiar books, ones that have been read aloud to them once, twice, or a hundred times, the meaning is set and tied to their experiences of listening to an adult read it aloud to them. For example, children who have heard *Knuffle Bunny* before will always read it with the same meaning and story line in mind. It will forever be the story of Trixie going to the Laundromat with her dad, leaving her stuffed bunny there, realizing it, and then pitching a fit until the mother realizes the problem, which ultimately resolves itself nicely.

Once children know a picture book, they cannot "un-know" it. A child who has heard *Knuffle Bunny* a few times is much less likely to create an alternative story line, such as Trixie washed Knuffle Bunny on purpose because it was so dirty, or that she was crying because she was tired after walking so far and doing laundry, or that she missed her mommy, so her dad took her home, but she wanted to have her Knuffle Bunny for her nap, so they had to go back to get it. This alternative story is quite possible for a child who is reading *Knuffle Bunny* for the first time. The illustrations and pictures, as well as the child's schema, could support this alternative. When a text is unfamiliar, children have the opportunity to use their resourcefulness to figure out the story as they go, and they have the chance to use lots of strategies along the way.

As Wade turned the pages of *Zoom*, he was quite resourceful and scrappy in his efforts to understand what was going on in the story. Without the assistance or enabling of an adult, Wade had to rely on and integrate both his schema, including life experiences and knowledge, with the meaning he made from the illustrations to understand what was happening in the text. Young readers are called upon to infer characters' intentions and feelings, determine importance as they look closely at illustrations, and use all they know about how texts go and how they sound to read an unfamiliar book. Because they are constructing meaning without the aid of an adult's prior reading of the text, young children have to initiate and rely on a wide range of comprehension strategies to figure out how to read each page.

YOUNG CHILDREN PROBLEM-SOLVE INDEPENDENTLY AND TAKE MANAGED RISKS AS THEY EXPLORE A SAFE UNKNOWN.

Learners need two things to acquire skill, proficiency, and automaticity with any new task—whether they're learning to quilt, to belly dance, to build wooden boats, to sing Gregorian chants, to solve quadratic equations, to walk on a slack line—they need opportunities to independently orchestrate all of the strategies they've learned and they need opportunities to problem-solve on their own. When a child tries to read an unfamiliar book, he is called on to do both of these things—he needs to use everything he knows and intuit about reading, while engaging in a self-initiated problem-solving task.

A typical challenge for young readers of unfamiliar books is finding a point of entry in a book they don't know. We've watched children approach unfamiliar books in a variety of ways as they figure out how to get into them. Some look through the book to get a sense of the whole text before reading it, whereas other children jump right in and read the pictures and illustrations with little hesitation. Yet other children are reluctant and wary if they don't have prior experiences with the book that have been mediated by an adult. In the case of young and hesitant readers, we've realized that it is rather easy to nudge them to read unfamiliar texts, and very quickly their hesitation can change to enthusiasm for the task. We'll share ways to help children read unfamiliar books strategically and enthusiastically in the next chapter where we discuss conferring with children as they read unfamiliar books.

Another challenge arises when children realize, sometimes all of a sudden, that the pictures and illustrations don't support their reading of the book. In other words, in the case of a narrative text, children may read a text with a particular story line until an illustration contradicts their interpretation. When this happens, children can either choose to continue on with their reading despite the dissonance, or they might decide to go back to reread and retrace their steps through the text in an attempt to self-correct. The willingness to proceed through difficulty and the patience to start again are helpful life skills to acquire, and making efforts to fix any problem is a crucial reading skill to develop.

YOUNG CHILDREN DEVELOP STAMINA TO STAY WITH A CHALLENGING TASK AND HONE THEIR ABILITIES TO STAY FOCUSED.

When young children pick up an unknown book, they don't have a previous "read" to rely upon. They are blazing a trail through an unexplored book rather than walking along a well-traveled pathway. This requires engagement and persistence. Children need stamina and focus to get from the beginning to the end of an unfamiliar book.

The work that children do in unfamiliar texts is challenging. As is the case with any new and difficult activity, whether it's running a hilly route for the first time, taking on an intricate knitting project, or learning a new song on the guitar for your father's eightieth birthday party, there are moments in the challenge when it's tempting to give up—you feel tired, you feel frustrated, you feel the reward isn't worth the effort.

It's these times when you want to run back down the hill and over to your tried-and-true (and flat) running route; it's when you say, "Ugh. Forget it. I can't knit gloves," and you go back to knitting scarves as presents; it's when you toss away the new sheet music and end up playing your old stand-by, "Smoke on the Water," at your dad's party even though he used to yell at you for playing it so loud when you were a teenager. Despite the challenges encountered in these examples, the runner, the knitter, and the guitar player are actually doing activities that are familiar, albeit they're doing them in new ways.

Well, it's the same for our youngest children when they have an unfamiliar book on their laps. They are doing a familiar thing—reading a book—yet it's also challenging, frustrating, tiring, and (hopefully) rewarding because they are matching a familiar task—reading a book—with a new challenge—reading an unfamiliar book.

When a child picks out an unfamiliar book to read, it helps when we can provide reassurance and strategies to help the her overcome that initial impulse to give up and go onto something else. On the other hand, when a child eagerly takes on the work and play of figuring out what's going on in an unfamiliar book, we can be supportive by giving him tips and tricks for figuring out what might be happening and holding on to the meaning across the pages.

Characteristics of Unfamiliar Books That Invite Children to Do Big Thinking

We're like many people who have favorite restaurants; we also have favorite menu choices. When we go to these restaurants, we usually choose to order what's tried-and-true, our go-to dish, a menu item we know and love. Even if we're tempted by a particular special or in the mood for something new, we often talk ourselves out of it to enjoy the comfort and safety of the familiar choice. When we do choose something we've never tried before, the conditions have to be just right. We have to be motivated to try something new, our interest in the new item has to be piqued for some reason, and the dish has to meet certain criteria, such as containing or not containing certain ingredients. There are some similar conditions that seem to hold true when children choose to venture into an unfamiliar book rather than choosing a tried-and-true familiar book.

> # Children need opportunities and motivation to pick unfamiliar books.
>
> We provide opportunities for children to choose unfamiliar books when we have lots of books in our classrooms and in our homes. Having the books is only one part, however. We also have to make time for children to explore them and we need to air our expectations and hopes that they will do so. In other words, the act of reading an unfamiliar text cannot, itself, be unfamiliar. It needs to be a regular part of a young child's day, and when she makes the choice to trailblaze through a new book, we are wise to celebrate it.

THE TEXT IS INTERESTING AND ACCESSIBLE TO STUDENTS.

Unfortunately, the most important characteristic—that the book is interesting to children—is hard to predict and tricky to guarantee. It's helpful when teachers and parents know the topical interests, passions, and sensibilities of their children and use this knowledge to find books for their classrooms and homes. Even when we fill our bookshelves with consideration of our children's interests, children can be fickle or surprising in their tastes. Every teacher has had the experience in which one class absolutely loves a particular book, and the next year's class has no interest at all in that book. Kathy worked with Julian, a child who loved baseball and talked about it all the time with classroom buddies, with custodians, with anyone within earshot, actually. She dutifully filled a basket with picture books with baseball story lines and informational texts about baseball, biographies, sports almanacs, and so on, yet neither Julian nor his friends ever read anything from this basket.

Although our best attempts at matchmaking kids and books might fail at times, we are charmed when they gravitate toward books we would never have predicted. That year, Julian fell in love with an old tattered copy of *I'll Be You and You'll Be Me*, by Ruth Krauss and Maurice Sendak. This book began as an unfamiliar read for Julian and very quickly became a go-to book, one he loved to read with friends. So although it can be hard to predict which books will attract our children, it's worth our while to offer a big range of unfamiliar books that have some characteristics supportive of young readers.

THE ILLUSTRATIONS ARE DETAILED ENOUGH FOR A CHILD TO MAKE MEANING ACROSS PAGES, YET NOT TOO DETAILED THAT IT CAN BE HARD TO FOLLOW MEANING ACROSS THE TEXT.

Because children don't have an adult's prior reading of the text to lean on, they depend on the pictures and illustrations to help them figure out what's going on. For this reason, it's helpful when the child can build meaning, one illustration to the next. The Pigeon series by Mo Willems is very popular, but the books wouldn't be supportive unfamiliar texts for a child trying to read. Although the books are very engaging, the pictures don't provide enough detail for a child to make inferences and to build a through-line, in our experience. This is not to say that we wouldn't invite children to read Pigeon books, whether or not we had read them aloud. If a child chooses to read a Pigeon book on her own, of course, we would support her efforts.

On the other hand, when the illustrations have many details or when they are very busy, visually speaking, it can be hard for a child to figure out how to find the connections across the pages. Richard Scarry books offer an example of this characteristic. Although many children love the little scenes that fill pages and they enjoy spotting idiosyncrasies in the abundant details, these books can be difficult for children to navigate on their own. For one thing, it can be hard to them to figure out where to start their eyes on the pages. Again, we would never dissuade a child from choosing Richard Scarry's books or others with highly detailed illustrations, but we do acknowledge that texts like these are challenging for a child to create meaning or make inferences across pages.

THE ILLUSTRATIONS CONTAIN CHARACTERS WHO LOOK LIKE THEY ARE SAYING SOMETHING.

When a child sees characters talking in a text, she can imagine what the characters might be saying. This gives the child opportunities to infer characters' words, motivations, feelings, and thoughts. When a child reads a book like *Knuffle Bunny* for the first time, and before any adult has read it to him, he is likely to use visual cues that suggest the characters are talking (open mouths, positioning on the pages, talk bubbles, emotional facial expressions) and then infer what they might be saying using all the rest of the cues the illustrations offer.

THERE ARE SOME CONSISTENT ELEMENTS IN MOST OF THE ILLUSTRATIONS.

The most helpful consistent element is when the same characters live on page after page. When a child reads a book like *Knuffle Bunny* for the first time, it helps that the characters appear on most of the pages. This consistency helps a young reader carry and develop her meaning and interpretation of the text from one page to the next. Another helpful consistent element is if the illustrations use the same settings throughout the text. A book like *Wemberly Worried* by Kevin Henkes that moves between home and school is supportive because the child doesn't have to acclimate the meaning he is making to new or one-time settings.

In the next chapter, we'll suggest ideas for what to say and how to support children when they make the brave choice to trailblaze and read an unfamiliar book.

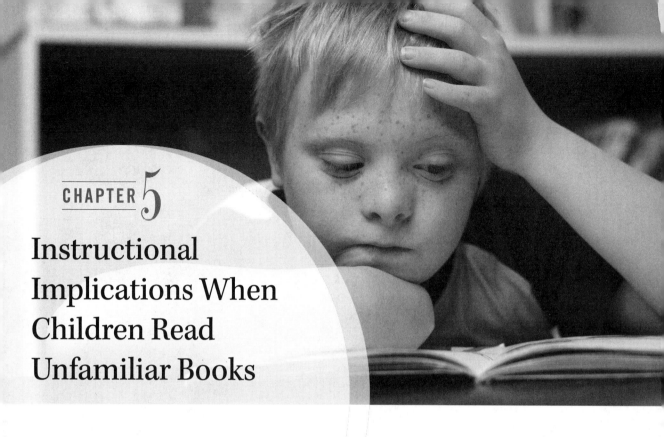

CHAPTER 5

Instructional Implications When Children Read Unfamiliar Books

*I*n a kindergarten class in early September, Michael pulled *Wink: The Ninja Who Wanted to Take a Nap* from a tabletop book bin. Before opening the book, he paused to look closely at the cover and said to himself, "I love ninjas." Michael quickly flipped through the first couple of pages and, without comment, put the book back into the basket. We asked him why he put the book back so quickly. He said, "I can't read it." Even very young children believe that knowing exactly what the words say is the one and only right way to read a book. Consequently, before they are able to read conventionally, children might regard books that nobody has ever read to them before as off-limits or inaccessible. Michael, and so many other children, just need to know a few easily learned strategies so they can effectively and confidently interact with books they haven't heard read aloud before.

This is an important thing to learn how to do. After all, children will encounter unfamiliar books everywhere. They fill bookcases and baggies, tabletop bins and center baskets. They're shelved in classroom libraries, school libraries, independent bookstores, and doctors' offices. They're found at friends' houses, stoop sales, garage sales, and so on. Most of the texts that young children encounter will be unfamiliar to them. If children are reluctant to choose unfamiliar books and unaware of ways they can read them to themselves, they will miss out on valuable experiences and opportunities as readers. It's crucial that we provide support for children so they become enthusiastic about turning the pages of unfamiliar texts wherever they find them, and so they feel empowered to make meaning in any book they're holding.

By providing both the opportunity to navigate unfamiliar texts as well as the instructional support to do this successfully, we open up new frontiers for young children's reading explorations.

As we observed and conferred with children who were interacting with unfamiliar texts, we quickly realized that there are simple nudges and quick supports we could provide that would offer huge benefits to the child. Although some children may have started their reading with hesitation and uncertainty, these supports and nudges quickly helped them grow more confident and independent as they moved through unfamiliar texts. In most cases, after we showed children a variety of strategies to help figure out what was going on in unfamiliar texts, we watched as they transferred these strategies to their independent reading of other unfamiliar books.

By providing both the opportunity to navigate unfamiliar texts as well as the instructional support to do this successfully, we open up new frontiers for young children's reading explorations. Children who only chose books or characters that they knew very well began to opt for books and characters that they had never seen before. Children who were reluctant to read an unfamiliar book in the company of others quickly became willing to share their new finds with their friends.

To support and nudge children as they read unfamiliar texts, we begin by figuring out what they already know how to do and what they already believe about reading. We figure out what they aren't doing yet. We ask ourselves, "What's the next thing this child might need, given where the child is right now?"

In a process that was similar to the way we studied children reading familiar texts, we observed language use as children negotiated the meaning in these unfamiliar texts. We realized that, just like with familiar books, there were different levels of independence (see Chapter 7) and different degrees of sophistication of children's language use that we've turned into Unfamiliar Books Language Levels.

We present these Unfamiliar Books Language Levels with the same concerns we felt in sharing Familiar Books Language Levels in Chapter 3. We acknowledge that there's an inherent risk in detailing levels and creating categories, rubrics, and continua, especially when they are used to label, rank, score, or categorize young children's work. As we mentioned earlier, our intention in naming language levels isn't to quantify young children's preconventional reading with a level but rather to use the descriptions of the levels to inform our instruction so we can best support children's reading before they're decoding.

Another challenge with creating levels for preconventional reading work is that children don't operate in the tidy world of clearly delineated levels. In most cases, they don't fit neatly into one category. Rarely are we able to pinpoint a date that a child moved from one level to another because growth is gradual over time, and children often zigzag backward and forward in the short term with any text.

In other words, we've found that children are rarely only "one way" and they constantly cross categories. They may sit on the cusp between one level and another, depending on the text. They may present characteristics of a particular level in one text, but then they read in a way that's characteristic of another level in a different text. They may display behaviors and express themselves in ways that draw from more than one language level within a single book!

So with these caveats and concerns in mind once again, we're going to share another set of language levels that are meant to help us see possibilities for supporting children, this time for when children are reading unfamiliar texts.

Unfamiliar Book Language Level 1

When children read a book that nobody has ever read aloud to them before, they tend to pause at the illustrations in their efforts to infer meaning. Similar to readers of familiar books, children at this language level with unfamiliar books look at the picture and say what they see. This might include pointing and labeling the people, objects, and actions on the page. Typically, their descriptions of characters, objects, and actions are sparse.

Sometimes a child operating in this language level may use her schema of another text she knows to make meaning in the unfamiliar one (Figure 5.1). She might see a wolf in an illustration in the unfamiliar book and call him the "big bad wolf" because of her knowledge of the wolf in *The Three Little Pigs*, regardless of whether the wolf in the story she is reading at that moment is actually big and bad.

Clip 5.1 *Jake Reads* Dogs *(Unfamiliar)*
http://smarturl.it/Clip5.1

Unfamiliar Book Language Level 1

Description	Sample Transcript
• The child attends to pictures and illustrations. • The child names and labels objects without elaboration. • The child may not connect one page to another.	Child reading **Knuffle Bunny:** Pointing to parts of the picture: "A baby. Her mommy is waving. Her daddy. She has a doll. / The girl and her daddy. That man is reading."

Figure 5.1

We invite you to watch Jake read an excerpt of *Dogs,* a picture book with a list structure that he's never heard before, although he has looked through the book once. Jake begins by pointing to and naming dogs that are illustrated in the inside cover ("Fire doggie, spots dog, girl dog, girl dog, big boy dog, another dog . . ."). When he gets to the first page, he reads exactly what he sees on the page, "Dog bone and a ball." As he continues through the book, he does this same thing, naming how the dogs look or what the dogs are doing on each page ("Mad doggie, very bad doggie . . . nobody fighting . . . dusty."). Jake provides very little elaboration as he reads, nor does he ever move beyond labeling the pictures.

Unfamiliar Book Language Level 2

In Unfamiliar Book Language Level 2, children begin to elaborate more as they notice and name what they see in the illustrations. Instead of saying, "Dog bone and a ball," the child might read, "The big dog is playing with his ball. There's a dog bone, too." They build on the characteristics seen in Unfamiliar Book Language Level 1, as their language around the text becomes richer and more complex. In addition to elaborating more when reading, this is the stage in which children begin to make more inferences about what they see (Figure 5.2). For example, they might:

- Infer how the characters are feeling. ("She's mad at him!")
- Infer about events and actions that aren't immediately obvious from the illustrations. (Instead of looking at the illustration and saying, "They're playing soccer," the child might infer and say, "The blue guy has the ball. He's going to score!")

- Infer to create dialogue. If the book has characters who interact, the child may imagine the dialogue, usually based on what is happening in the book. This dialogue could be in the third person (e.g., the child points to the character and says, "He's saying, 'I'm sorry'") or first person as the child speaks in the voice of the character (e.g., the child points to the character and says, "I'm sorry!"). In these examples, the child has inferred that the character is sorry based on facial expressions, gestures, or events in the illustrations.
- Assume the role of the character. Although many children might describe character actions in the third person (i.e., "He's building a tower"), some children take on the persona of the character and say, "I'm building a tower now." Still other children might give the character a name (i.e., "Jesse is knocking down the tower") or other signifier (i.e., "Her brother is going to knock down her tower").

Clip 5.2 *Wade Reads* Biscuit *(Unfamiliar)*

http://smarturl.it/Clip5.2

In the video of Wade, we observe as he reads a Biscuit book. He has never read this book before, which he states emphatically, although he is familiar with the Biscuit series. As Wade turns the pages, he uses connecting words such as *and* or *and then* as he goes to the next page. Instead of just saying there's a dog on the page and naming what the dog is doing, Wade uses more details and elaborates on what he reads in the illustration.

Unfamiliar Book Language Level 2

Description	Sample Transcript
• *The child attends to pictures and illustrations.* • *The child names and labels objects, with some elaboration and details.* • *The child tries to connect one page to the next using words like **and** or **and then**.* • *The child infers characters' feelings and text events that aren't on the page.* • *The child might imagine character dialogue.*	Child reading ***Knuffle Bunny***: *"The mom is waving 'bye-bye' to the girl and her daddy. They are going with their laundry basket. And the girl has her doll. A bunny, I think. / The girl walks with her dad / and they walk in the park."*

Figure 5.2

Unfamiliar Book Language Level 3

At this level, children's language and inferences become more sophisticated. They use literary language and syntax by activating their schema for how books tend to go. Rather than naming what's on each page, at this level children elaborate more and offer some editorial comments as they linger longer on the illustrations. We've noticed that their prosody and expression sound more like they are reading conventionally. In many cases, they are actively trying to make their reading sound like they're really reading the words. In some cases, the children may locate a word or two and use it to anchor their reading (Figure 5.3).

Clip 5.3 *Aliah Reads* **Roller Coaster** *(Unfamiliar)*

http://smarturl.it/Clip5.3

As we watch Aliah read *Roller Coaster*, we observe that her sentences are longer and filled with inferential thinking. She says, "People are going up there so they could go on the roller coaster because some people got on it and they didn't have a turn. They're on the

Unfamiliar Book Language Level 3

Description	Sample Transcript
• The child attends to pictures and illustrations. • The child elaborates more on each page. It sounds like he's reading more sentences per page, instead of one line per page. • The child uses text sense and literary language to connect one page to another. • The child infers characters' feelings and text events that aren't on the page. • The child imagines what characters might say. • The child editorializes about the text.	Child reading **Knuffle Bunny**: "One day a girl and her daddy are going with their laundry. The mom says 'Bye bye, don't forget to do the laundry.' The girl has her stuffed animal with her, and it's a bunny. / The girl and her daddy are walking and walking. They go down the street and they're holding hands. / They go in the park and the girl is running fast. Daddy said, 'Wait for me!'! The girl said, 'You can't catch me!'"

Figure 5.3

roller coaster. They're getting on there, but that little girl is scared." She goes on to explain to Matt that she knows the girl is scared because of the expression on her face. She spends more time studying the illustrations for details that she incorporates into her reading.

As we looked through our video footage and worked with children reading unfamiliar texts, we realized over and over that children are rarely ever perfectly "level-able" as they read unfamiliar books (or familiar ones for that matter). Sometimes, a child might start an unfamiliar book with an Unfamiliar Book Language Level 1 approach, but as he turns the pages, he begins to better understand the story. As his understanding expands, the language he uses to read the story increases.

Alternatively, a child may begin reading a book in a way that is characteristic of Unfamiliar Book Language Level 2 or 3, and as she proceeds through the text, her stamina might wane because of the effort involved with making meaning throughout an unfamiliar text. She may lose focus and revert to a language default position in which she begins to just name the characters or objects on the pages.

As we support children while they're reading unfamiliar books, it helps so much to be aware of the characteristics of the different language levels. It's important to teach with agility, moving our nudges and instruction, even within one book, to accommodate the variety of ways children may be reading, again, even within one book.

Conferring to Support Students Within and to Nudge Students Across Levels

The child's initial moments with the unfamiliar book are critical. If the book holds the child's interest, and if the child is confident in her abilities to navigate an unfamiliar book, she is more likely to dive in. On the other hand, if a child is more conscientious of reading the "right way," or more reliant on the book being previously read by an adult, he may be less likely to commit to reading something that's unfamiliar.

Although Wade was ready to read *Zoom* right away even though it was unfamiliar to him, other children might be more like Tarah, another preschool-age child that we observed. Tarah didn't want to read *Let's Go, Hugo*, even though she chose that one from an assortment of books. She looked at the first few pages and then closed the book. "I don't know how to read it," she said, leaning back to push her chair from the table.

Tarah may have found reading an unfamiliar book to be a high-frustration and low-reward task, so she tried to quickly abandon it. When this is the case, how fortunate it would be if we were sitting alongside that child. We could support and nudge her toward reading the text by saying, "Oh, I see you're reading *Let's Go, Hugo*. Do you know this story?" When Tarah shakes her head no, we could say, "Oh, no problem. It's fun to figure out a new book. You know what I do? I like to figure it out by looking closely at the pictures. Let's try it together."

We've learned that when children initially hesitate, resist, or downright refuse to read before they can read conventionally, it's really rather easy to show them that they can, in fact, read. In almost every situation when a child hesitated at the beginning, it didn't take very much prompting or support for the child to give it a try.

We've found it's helpful to start by acknowledging the underlying issue. Some children may harbor a real and genuine concern that they don't know how to read "the right way" or they're worried they won't be able to do what you want them to do. So instead of responding with animated and encouraging words, like "You can read this. Just give it a try!" or "C'mon. You can read it!" we've learned that we need to meet them where they are, in the land of uncertainty, by inviting them to find their way into the text. The next step is to show them how (Figure 5.4).

We invite you to watch Matt confer with Neve, a four-year-old. Neve chose to read a book about horses that nobody had ever read aloud to her before. When Matt asked her if she would read it to him, she said, "Yeah," without any moment of hesitation or hint of reluctance. Interestingly, earlier that day, Neve told Matt that she *couldn't* read a book when he asked her to do so. In between that morning interaction and her afternoon willingness to read, her teacher had read aloud a new book to the class.

Some Humble Beginnings of Unfamiliar Book Conferences

Child May Say Something Like	We Can Say Things in Response, Such As
"I can't read this." "I don't know how to read this." "I don't know this book." "You read it to me." "You have to read it." "No."	"Oh, is this the first time you're reading this? Great! You get to figure it out! It helps to really look closely at the pictures. Let's try it together." "There are lots of ways to read a book. Are you four? You know, you can read it in a four- or even a five-year-old way by reading the pictures. Let me show you what I mean." "When I don't know a book, the first thing I do is explore it. Let's look through it and see what might be going on. We can look at the pictures, and we can say what we see, like this . . ."

Figure 5.4

Neve begins by attending to a rip in the page, which Matt talks about with her for a moment because that's what's holding her attention. Then as Neve begins to read, she points to a word and asks, "What's this word?" (The words are in the form of labels for the body parts of the horse.) Matt asks her what she thinks it is and prompts her to notice what it's pointing to as a clue to help her figure it out. When Neve doesn't respond immediately, Matt says, "Those are the ears," and then he points to another label. Matt asks, "What are these down here?" Neve responds quickly, saying, "Legs." It's worth noting that Matt chose "legs" because Neve would likely know that body part, whether or not she has any schema about horses.

Once Neve gets how these labels work, she names other parts of the horse on that page in a way that sounds like labeling. As she turns the page, she continues reading with one-word labeling. After two pages, Neve independently moves to name the action when she says, "Horse running?" to which Matt responds, "Horse is running." Neve settles on that illustration longer than any that she had seen before. She expresses more details with a self-correction ("And people, two people are on it!") and offers some editorial comments ("I never saw that before!"). When she says this, Matt asks her to clarify. This gives Neve an opportunity to use more language as she talks about this text and her thoughts.

One characteristic that stands out in this conference is that Matt is a very patient observer, listening closely and waiting to find opportunities to support Neve. He didn't start out by setting an agenda for their time together but he listened to her and taught her the next thing she could do—say more about the pictures on the pages.

The other important thing Matt did was to pause Neve part of the way through the book to name the ways she's changed: "You said you couldn't read this. Then you read this. Now you're saying more as you read." Her confidence and motivation are increased through genuine feedback about what she was doing and how she grew, rather than vague and general comments like "Nice job." At this point, he essentially says something like "Now that you can do all this, here's something else to try." He's building off what she's shown she can do, and instead of redirecting her by teaching her something new, he chose to show her how to deepen the work that she's already begun.

CONFERRING: UNFAMILIAR BOOK LANGUAGE LEVEL 1

When we're working with children who read unfamiliar texts in a way that is mostly aligned with Unfamiliar Book Language Level 1 characteristics, often our priority is to support the child to use as much language as she can to name what she sees in the pictures (Figure 5.5).

CONFERRING: UNFAMILIAR BOOK LANGUAGE LEVEL 2

When young readers have moved beyond the one- and two-word labeling of texts, our work is to support them toward elaboration. We want to help them move from two- or three-word statements ("They are walking. There's a dog.") to include more details and descriptive language ("They are walking through the park, and there's a dog walking, too. He's going fast!"). We can also help them to imagine dialogue between characters, when this suits the text they are reading (Figure 5.6).

CONFERRING: UNFAMILIAR BOOK LANGUAGE LEVEL 3

When children read unfamiliar books in what we call Language Level 3, they elaborate more consistently, and we can add to their repertoire by teaching them to include more literary language and transitional words between pages. At this point, we'll want to give the child strategies to make the transitions between pages sound smoother and to help the child integrate more literary syntax and book-specific vocabulary rather than simply relying on her own oral language patterns to represent what might be happening in the text (Figure 5.7).

We've realized that it might take children two or three passes through the book before they reach Unfamiliar Book Language Level 3. The first read through the book often serves to orient children to the text. They get an overview and overall sense of how the text goes. On this first pass-through, most children tend to operate mostly in Unfamiliar Book Language Level 1. On each successive read, we've found that it can be easier to nudge them toward more elaboration and toward a more sophisticated literary reading of a text. Even though they are growing more familiar with the text on each read, we still consider the text unfamiliar because they don't know for sure what the text says. Nobody has ever read it to them before, so an actual and accurate reading of the text is not accessible.

When children have regular opportunities to read books that are unfamiliar, as well as expectations that they can do so, the wide world of books truly opens up to them. Once they have strategies to make meaning in books nobody has read to them before, children have access to any text they are interested in reading, even if they can't read the words.

Unfamiliar Book Language Level 1

Examples of What a Child Might Do While Reading	What Might We Do or Say to Support or Nudge This Child?	Example of an Interaction Between Child and Adult (Knuffle Bunny by Mo Willems)
• Stares at the first pages, not saying anything	• We can let the child know there are lots of ways to read a book. • We can tell the child the title and talk about the cover a bit. • We can give a very quick summary or overview of the text, if we know it. • We can model how to talk off of the picture.	Adult: (looking at the cover) "This book is called **Knuffle Bunny**! Look. I think that's Knuffle Bunny. What are you noticing?" Child: (points to Trixie) Adult: "The girl? The girl is holding Knuffle Bunny. What else do you notice?" Child: "Who's that?" Adult: "I think it's her daddy. It looks like this will be about a girl and her stuffed animal, Knuffle Bunny."
• Names and labels characters and/or objects with one or two words	• We can ask what the characters/objects are doing to help the child move from one- or two-word labeling to sentences and toward more elaboration. • We can encourage the child to name more things that she sees on the pages. • We can model full sentences and elaboration. (These prompts are similar to those for Familiar Books Language Level 1)	Child: "A girl and a daddy." Adult: "Yeah, there's Trixie and her daddy. Let's think about and say what they're doing together." Child: "Walking?" Adult: "Trixie and her daddy are walking down the street. Can you read this next page by telling everything you see?" Child: "They go in the park and there's a guy and a dog and it's a park."
• Attends to pictures and illustrations and makes editorial comments about them	• We can help the child connect his thinking to the story or we can support the child toward elaborating on his ideas and thinking. • We can model how to bring random ideas back to the text.	Child: "I have a animal too." Adult: "A stuffed animal, like Knuffle Bunny?" Child: (nods) Adult: "Are you like this child? Do you take your stuffed animal everywhere like Trixie does?" Child: "Yeah, I carry it." Adult: "You're like Trixie in this book. She's taking Knuffle Bunny on a walk down the street" (turns page and looks at child as if to say, "Your turn"). Child: "The park?" Adult: "Through the park . . ."

Figure 5.5

Unfamiliar Books Language Level 2

Examples of What a Child Might Do While Reading	What Might We Do or Say to Support or Nudge This Child?	Example of an Interaction Between Child and Adult (Knuffle Bunny by Mo Willems)
Names objects and actions with a little more detail	• We can encourage the child to build this into a couple of sentences about the pictures. • We can model how to do this. • We can go along with the child's interpretation of events even if they aren't accurate to the actual story if there's evidence in the illustrations to back up the child's interpretation. We're showing the child ways he can read anything on his own, and when he's reading on his own, before he can read conventionally, he may not always have an accurate interpretation of the story.	Child: "The daddy and the girl are going." Adult: "Yeah, I wonder where they're going? The daddy is carrying a laundry basket in his hand. Do you know what that is?" Child: (shakes head) Adult: "It has dirty clothes in it. They're going to wash the clothes. Now let's tell what they're doing." Child: "The daddy and the girl are going to wash the clothes." Adult: (taps picture near mom on stoop) Child: "And the mommy is waving." Adult: "So let's read the whole page and say everything we see." Child: "The girl and her daddy are going to wash the clothes. They have the clothes and the daddy has them. The mommy is waving to them."
Attends to character(s) across pages and states what the character(s) are doing or states details about the character	• We can encourage the child to infer what characters might be saying to each other or to infer how characters might be feeling by attending to facial expressions, gestures, and so on. • We can support the child to infer about what's going on in the text.	Child: "The girl and her daddy are going to wash the clothes and the mommy is waving." Adult: "Yeah, look at her face! It looks like she's saying something. What might she be saying to them?" Child: "Bye-bye." Adult: "Let's pretend we're the characters. I'll be the daddy and you can be the mommy. 'OK, we're going to the Laundromat to do the laundry and wash the clothes. See you later!'" Child: "'Bye-bye.'" Adult:" 'Bye-bye, see you later!'" Child: "'Bye-bye, see you later!'" Adult: "Look at the girl's face. How does she look?" Child: "Happy?" Adult: "Happy. What makes you think so?" Child: "She's smiling, and she's like this" (mimics her expression). *Continues*

Figure 5.6

Examples of What a Child Might Do While Reading	What Might We Do or Say to Support or Nudge This Child?	Example of an Interaction Between Child and Adult (Knuffle Bunny by Mo Willems)
Makes statements about their interpretations of the actions and feelings they see in the pictures	• We can ask the child to explain or show what in the picture gives her a particular idea. ("What makes you think she's sad?" "Why do you think they're having an argument?" "How do you know they're going on the roller coaster?")	Child: "The girl and her daddy are going back home (turns page). Uh-oh." Adult: "What's 'uh-oh'?" Child: (points to Trixie's face) Adult: "What are you thinking?" Child: "She's sad or something?" Adult: "What makes you think so?" Child: "Her eyes are like this" (mimics Trixie's saucer-shaped eyes). Adult: "What happened? On this page (turns back) Trixie looks like happy like 'la di da we're walking home' and now she's like this" (mimics Trixie's expression). Child: "Now she looks scared or something." Adult: "I wonder why. Let's try to figure it out" (goes back a few pages and retells with child).

Figure 5.6 (Continued)

Unfamiliar Book Language Level 3

Examples of What a Child Might Do While Reading	What Might We Do or Say to Support or Nudge This Child?	Example of an Interaction Between Child and Adult (Knuffle Bunny by Mo Willems)
Continues building on the skills of Unfamiliar Book Language Level 1 and Unfamiliar Book Language Level 2 Attends to pictures and illustrations Names objects and actions with more text-based detail and story language Starts to connect one page to another to create a cohesive reading	• We can continue to support the child in elaborating more and sharing his thinking about the texts. • We can support the child in reading with expression and prosody. • We can continue to model full sentences and elaboration as well as cohesive reading across pages. • We can add literary language to a child's reading. • We can encourage the child to use what she knows about how books go, literary language, and so on to help her reading sound more like a cohesive text.	Child: "Daddy said, 'OK, baby, we're all done now. Let's go.' So they walked home. The daddy was whistling like this (whistle sounds). Then Trixie got sad. Then she told her daddy with baby words." Adult: "You want to try something? Should we try to make it sound just like a story? Watch this. I'll try it first and then you try it. 'OK, baby, let's go home,' said Daddy. So he and his baby walked home. The daddy whistled a happy tune and the baby looked around happily, until all of a sudden…" (turns to child). Child: "All of a sudden the baby got sad, and she told her daddy with baby words." Adult: "How would she sound?" Child: "Blah blah blah?" Adult: "Yeah, but sadder, right. Look at her face… let's see, all of a sudden, the baby got sad and she said to her daddy…" Child: (more expressively) "Blah blah blah… but her daddy didn't know what she said. And the baby got sadder and sadder."

Figure 5.7

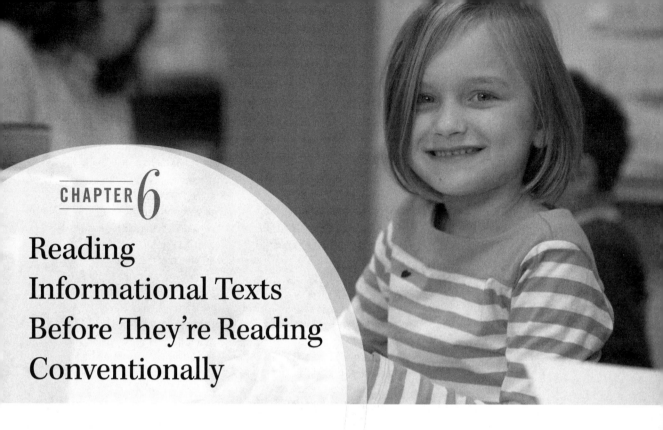

CHAPTER 6

Reading Informational Texts Before They're Reading Conventionally

Mikey and his two buddies, Alex and Daniel, walked into their kindergarten classroom one Monday morning chattering about the Indianapolis Colts' victory the night before. After hanging their coats and book bags in their cubby, they spread out around the room to start their day. Alex headed straight to the fish tank to record some observations—he was the class pet vet for the month. Daniel went to the block area to check on a structure he and some friends had started the week before. Mikey paused in front of the SMART Board, his eyes locked on the day's schedule. His shoulders slumped and he said, "Aw, man!" to nobody in particular. Jenny, his teacher, heard this and headed over.

Jenny knelt down beside Mikey. "Hey, what's going on?" she asked. Pointing to the day's schedule, he said, "I forgot my library book." She assured him that Mrs. Bernard, the school librarian, would let him choose a book to put on reserve until he returned the one he forgot.

That was little consolation—Mikey explained how he and Alex were planning ask Mrs. Bernard if they could swap books—Alex wanted the football book that Mikey had taken out last week, and Mikey wanted Alex's book about NFL quarterbacks. He and Alex had made a firm plan, and Mikey was upset that it wouldn't work out as they envisioned.

Jenny's class loves library time and looks forward to it each week. Even though Jenny has a well-stocked classroom library, there is something slightly free-range and exciting about looking for books in the school library. Mrs. Bernard, the librarian, often has brand-new books to share, and somehow she always makes good recommendations for books that align with whatever Jenny's class is studying.

Another appeal of the school library for Jenny's kindergartners is that they get to borrow books from the same shelves where the big kids find their books. Sometimes there's a class of fifth graders in the library at the same time, and Jenny's kindergartners stare wide-eyed as they watch the big kids fan out among the shelves trying to find what they want to read. When it's time for the kindergartners to look for books, they often find themselves standing side by side with big kids in the informational book section.

The relationship Jenny's children have with their school library is a typical one that plays out across schools and classrooms that are fortunate enough to have a well-resourced and well-used school library led by an engaged librarian. The children enter the library expectantly, scanning the shelf tops and mini book stands for the newest titles. "I see the new Pete the Cat!" Ayana says loudly after noticing the new book in the basket next to Mrs. Bernard's reading chair.

On this particular Monday, after listening to Mrs. Bernard read aloud a book about changes in nature during autumn, the kindergartners scattered among the shelves, searching for new books to take home. Two children immediately approached Mrs. Bernard to see if they could take home the book she had just read aloud to them. A few of the children headed straight for the picture book section, and the rest of the class headed directly to the shelves containing informational books. Michelle chose a horse book and sat down right away to read it, and Jackson looked through several truck and tractor books before picking the one he'd borrow for the week. Deshawn tilted his head sideways as he scanned the shelves containing books about sports. Meanwhile, Mikey sat next to Alex, looking through an Eyewitness Book about football. Mikey was waiting to take out the book about quarterbacks that Alex just returned.

What's striking here is not the engagement or the energy of library day or the concentration of children exploring informational texts. What stands out is the simple predictability of it. Many children gravitate naturally toward informational books, and they don't need a unit of study or a thematic study or a research assignment to inspire them to do so.

We considered folding this chapter about informational books into both the familiar and unfamiliar chapters. After all, many kids love to reread familiar informational books and to discover unfamiliar ones. There are many children who easily engage with informational books, whether or not someone has read them aloud before.

In the end, we decided that this work merits its own chapter, and not because there are emerging mandates and pressures—some soft and some firm—to increase the amount and sophistication of informational reading in the earliest grades. We believe that informational books are worthy of their own chapter because *children have shown us they are.*

We do acknowledge that there are some children (and adults) who don't have a natural attraction to informational texts. They may prefer story to exposition. They may prefer imaginary to informational. They may prefer happy endings to concluding paragraphs. We always respect children's tastes and preferences, yet it's also very important to help them find a wide variety of texts they can love. In our efforts to help children find themselves and their interests within informational texts, we strive to expose them to a wide variety of types and topics choices by reading aloud informational texts as often as we can, and then by giving children many opportunities to read them on their own.

This can be easier to say than to do, however. Research shows that until very recently most early childhood classrooms contained few informational texts and teachers devoted less time to reading aloud informational texts (Duke 2000). Many teachers and caregivers are more inclined to read aloud fictional picture books. These types of texts offer us obvious opportunities to read with expression and to engage with story. They're also somewhat more straightforward to read aloud because they are typically written to be read from cover to cover. Informational books can be trickier to read in an engaging and expressive way. The layout of an informational text page may not be a typical left-to-right, top-to-bottom read due to a variety of graphic elements. The effort of reading aloud informational texts involves a variety of macro and micro decisions on the part of the teacher. Additionally, the page layouts in many informational books make them difficult to read aloud to a whole class. The graphic elements might be hard for all children to see.

> *We always respect children's tastes and preferences, yet it's also very important to help them find a wide variety of texts they can love.*

Some teachers and caregivers may also wonder if their children will be able to understand informational texts, especially if they don't have a schema for the topic. Children's informational texts can contain specialized vocabulary and sophisticated concepts, and adults might worry that they'll lose children's interest and comprehension if they read these texts aloud. For these reasons, caregivers and teachers may not think to provide regular access to informational books, nor do they typically choose to read them aloud to their children, even if they are classrooms and homes with regular read-aloud times and abundant books. Conventional wisdom may suggest that narrative texts may be more developmentally appropriate for young children, but research shows that when they are given opportunities to explore informational books, young children have successful interactions with them (Duke 2003).

When exploring books beyond the walls of classrooms or home, young children typically have limited contact with informational texts. In children's sections of bookstores, for example, the titles that have the fanciest real estate and front-and-center display shelves are usually the newest picture books, the hottest authors, or the trendiest series, which may be exclusively fictional texts. Information books are often relegated to shelves off to the side. They're shelved "spine out" instead of in flashy face-out displays, which makes it hard for young children to find books they want to read.

Fortunately, this isn't usually the case in school libraries or public libraries. In our experience, school librarians are more likely to feature informational texts for children in a more front-and-center way, which is due, perhaps, to librarians' closer proximity to the lives and interests of the children in their community.

Benefits of Informational Books

There are many benefits when children begin their reading lives with opportunities to listen to informational texts read aloud as well as regular encouragement to read informational texts on their own. If children are exposed to and have access to a wide variety of informational texts from very early on, they will be more likely to pursue informational texts for their own reading pleasures and purposes.

We would like to take a moment at this point to acknowledge the educational elephant in the room. There has been a well-publicized push for increasing the quantity of informational texts in early childhood classrooms, largely due to the emphasis on this type of reading and writing in the Common Core State Standards. Many teachers across the country are held accountable for getting their children to meet these standards, so there has been more interest in finding ways to best support young children as they read and understand informational texts.

We are more interested in helping children to love books, to read widely, and to develop a lifelong enthusiasm for learning.

One problem with using the CCSS as the main rationale for increasing the time spent reading informational texts in early childhood classrooms is that, in our opinion, the standards for early childhood were not conceived with young children in mind—rather they were created to prepare young children to move through the grades to ultimately be college and career ready.

So, we want to be clear. We advocate for more informational book read-alouds and more opportunities for young children to explore informational books because it's good for children, not because of the CCSS. We are more interested in helping children to love books, to read widely, and to develop a lifelong enthusiasm for learning. As we wrote in the introduction, when we do things that are right for children, readiness is a by-product. It doesn't have to be the goal.

Reading aloud informational books to young children and providing opportunities for them to explore and read these texts on their own is important because children:

1. enjoy them and are motivated to read informational texts
2. learn content and acquire vocabulary from informational texts
3. develop a habit of using texts to pursue interests, to know more

ENTHUSIASM AND MOTIVATION TO READ

Children are naturally attracted to informational texts for a variety of reasons. Often, children develop a passion or curiosity about something that leads them to pursue texts on that topic. Valicia was five years old when she became obsessed with flowers. When her class grew marigolds for a science project, Valicia declared that she wanted to know the name of every flower in the world. Her mom fed her obsession through weekly library trips and frequent stops at the neighborhood community garden. Valicia studied the flowers on display at the corner store and began to name them out loud. At one point, Valicia's mom couldn't find enough books about flowers. "We've already borrowed all of the kids' flower books from the library," her mom said with exasperation. "I don't know what else to do. It's like she's a flower book addict!"

Valicia's teacher suggested that they might look through the adult gardening or art books sections. Valicia's mom said she was doubtful at first. "I thought that those books were for grown-ups. I didn't think they would be interesting for Valicia." Her doubts were unfounded, however. Valicia loved looking through the pictures in the adult gardening books. Valicia began to draw flowers inspired by the botanical sketches she saw in art books. She begged her mom to plant a window box garden. Who knows what direction this childhood passion for flowers and the intentional pursuit of information might take for Valicia as she grows as a learner and a reader?

Although Valicia pursued informational books to fuel an interest, some children might gravitate toward informational books because they're attracted to the illustrations and photographs. The graphic elements—pictures, illustrations, diagrams—serve as the informational text gateway for many children. The cover picture featuring a close-up of a koala bear in a tree may attract a child who, to this point, thought of koala bears only in the cute stuffed-animal sense and never considered the reality of koala bears. The two-page-spread photo collage of the world's most colorful and exotic beetles catches the eyes of a child who typically searches for Pete, the Cat books. Children often say that they like informational books because the pictures are of "real stuff."

Still other readers are attracted to informational books for a very simple reason: informational books offer information. Most children are naturally curious and they love to know about things. Informational texts fulfill that desire to know and to understand themselves and their world. So, unlike Valicia, who read informational texts because she had a strong interest and a singular focus on learning about flowers, there are also a great many readers who prefer informational texts because they read to know more, no matter the topic.

LEARN CONTENT AND ACQUIRE VOCABULARY

When adults read informational books aloud, we expose children to vocabulary and concepts, whether they're in the classroom library area listening to their teacher as she reads about clouds from an Eyewitness book or whether they're in their comfy reading chair sidled up to mom as she reads a picture book about animals taking care of their babies. In these settings, children learn new words and new concepts, and they have the chance to clear up their confusions as they listen and talk about informational books in the company of others.

According to research, exposure to new words doesn't automatically lead to acquisition of those words. Instead, exposure to new words combined with contextualized explanations and conversations about the words leads to vocabulary building. Young children are able to acquire and understand complex topics and vocabulary when they have regular opportunities to interact with informational books as well as time to talk about the books (Leung 2008).

DEVELOP A HABIT OF USING TEXTS TO PURSUE INTERESTS

The contemporary catchphrase "Google it" had a predecessor—"Let's look it up." For generations, when a learner wanted to know anything, from a word definition, to who was the highest paid baseball player before free agency, to how to build a chicken coop, to the history of mummies, she would turn to text—a dictionary, a magazine article about the effects of free agency, a how-to book for building animal shelters, and an encyclopedia entry about King Tutankhamen. These days, a swipe of our finger and a search engine instantly bring us that information and so much more. Still, in each case, we're required to read an informational text (or watch an informational video, which requires its own kind of literacy—visual literacy). The reading part has not gone away, although the delivery system may have changed.

It's not in the purview of this book to get into the merits of digital tools versus traditional paper texts. So we won't. We will say that it's empowering to realize that whenever you want to know about something, you can pursue your inquiry by reading about it. From the time children are young, we want to instill the habits of mind of being curious, wondering, asking questions, developing interests, clearing up confusions, sharing knowledge, and so much more. But the truth is that those habits of mind need a companion—a habit of action. People can pursue their curiosities, wonders, questions, interests, and confusions by reading texts (whether they're on paper or on a screen) and talking about that reading. We can model this daily in our classrooms and in our homes through regular interactions with all kinds of texts, including all kinds of informational books.

Informational Book Characteristics

Because of a recent standards-based emphasis on reading and writing more informational texts for all grades, publishing companies are taking advantage of these increased demands. There are more informational texts available than ever before. We won't suggest one publishing company's books over another's. However, we can share some general characteristics of informational texts that appeal to young children because we've been paying attention to the kinds of informational texts that are most sought after by and engaging for young children. Although there are no absolutely foolproof characteristics or easily stated tips we can offer, we have learned that some kinds of books fly off of the book shelves in classrooms and school libraries.

1. **Topics of interest to children—at that moment in time.** We'd like to share a cautionary tale. For two years in a row, the space book basket in Zoe's class was empty all the time. Zoe spent her own money over the summer buying more space books and replacing the ones that had been well loved. Yet the very next school year, the space book basket gathered dust, even though it was still prominently displayed. One or two books may have had a moment of popularity, but then, like a pop music one-hit wonder, outer space faded quietly away. Zoe did all sorts of marketing for that book basket, trying to create buzz, but as they say, you can lead kids to a book basket but you cannot make them read. Meanwhile, the year that space faded, children were enthusiastic to read about various kinds of small pets, because Harry got a guinea pig for his birthday and declared it to be the best pet in the land. We can't know for sure what texts or topics will trend from year to year, so the best we can do is to listen closely for what captures our children's interests and to find books, books, and more books.

2. **Books with a variety of graphic elements and engaging text.** Children are often attracted to the books that teachers and caregivers have already read aloud to them. When we read aloud informational texts in the hopes that they will become the books children choose for themselves, we've found it helpful it if there's not too much text on each page. Even though children aren't reading conventionally, they'll use their recall for how the text goes in combination with picture support to read it by themselves. If there's too much text in relation to picture support, or if the text is formatted in long blocks that fill a page, the children might have a hard time finding their way in to it.

It's also very helpful if the nonfiction author crafts the writing with vibrant language, such as sound words (i.e., "The rocket WHOOSHES out of its launching pad and up into space") or action words ("The dance of a bumblebee can be more like a waltz or a cha-cha, depending on what they are trying to do"). Well-crafted language helps children hold on to information when we read aloud and can help anchor them to the book when they're reading on their own.

Because graphic elements are often children's entry point into a book, especially books that nobody has read aloud to them yet, we give consideration to the kinds of illustrations, photographs, and diagrams that texts contain. Although they may not read the words, children can begin to read and interpret diagrams, charts, and measures of scale.

Reading Informational Text

We've observed many children reading informational books before they're able read conventionally, and we've noticed that there are some discrete language levels that have some similarities with the way children approach both familiar and unfamiliar books, as well as characteristics that are specific to reading informational texts.

INFORMATIONAL BOOK LANGUAGE LEVEL 1

At this level children's reading of an informational book sounds very similar to their reading of any other book at Language Level 1, whether it's familiar or unfamiliar. They start by labeling the objects or action pictures or describing (without elaboration) what they see on each page. At this language level, if you were to listen to a child reading without looking at the book yourself, you wouldn't know that he is reading an informational text because it sounds like he could be naming objects or actions in any kind of book (Figure 6.1).

Informational Book Language Level 1

Description	Sample Transcript
• The child attends to pictures and illustrations. • The child names and labels objects without elaboration. • The child may not connect one page to another. • The child's reading does not reveal any informational text schema.	Child reading *The ABCs of Plants*: (Pointing to photographs on a page) "A flower. A leaf. There's the dirt …"

Figure 6.1

Clip 6.1 *Alex Reads* Rockets and Spaceships *(Informational)*

http://smarturl.it/Clip6.1

Watch as Alex reads about rockets. Alex identifies letters and recognizes some high-frequency words, and this is where most of his attention is directed at first. One way to approach a conference with Alex would be to offer him a choice of only "just-right" texts (Fountas & Pinnell Level A, probably) based on the observation that he's beginning to attend to print and he has some sight word automaticity. Yet, if we limit his books to only those that he can attempt to read conventionally, we would effectively narrow the field of informational texts to a very small pool of books. We wonder, why restrict young children to a limited pool of books so early in their reading lives? When children are ready to read conventionally because *they're* ready (not because they're *supposed to be* ready), we would certainly honor that by providing them with books that support them as conventional readers. However, we believe that young children can do wonderful reading work in most any informational text because the graphic elements offer them the opportunity to make meaning and to learn content.

So, aside from what Alex is doing with letters, sounds, and words, his reading in this text has characteristics of Language Level 1, in that he is mostly labeling what he sees in the pictures. Alex is an English language learner, so we recognize that part of the issue here may be that he doesn't yet have the vocabulary or the schema to elaborate. If Alex were reading a book about a topic with which he had more familiarity, he may have read it differently. All of these considerations would affect the way we might confer with Alex if we were sitting beside him.

INFORMATIONAL BOOK LANGUAGE LEVEL 2

When a child reads at Informational Book Language Level 2, she elaborates about the objects and actions she sees on the pages and she begins to read in a way that sounds more like cohesive text, one page connecting to the next. She may begin to make inferences and editorialize about what she sees on the page. For example, if the text is about baby animals, she might say, "The baby tiger is next to her mommy. / The baby monkey is hugging her mommy in the tree," whereas at Level 1 she would have read it as, "There's a tiger. Another tiger. / A baby monkey. That's the mommy." Although children at Language Level 2 sound like they're reading a text rather than labeling pictures, they aren't yet reading in a way that sounds like an informational book. In other words, their reading may sound like a story about the topic rather than sharing information about the topic (Figure 6.2).

Informational Book Language Level 2

Description	Sample Transcript
• The child attends to pictures and illustrations. • The child names and labels objects with more elaboration. • At times, the child tries to read the text in a way that sounds like he's putting the information into a more cohesive whole. • The child may switch between reading the text and editorializing as she reads. • The child sounds like he is reading a story about the topic rather than conveying information. He doesn't yet sound like he is reading informational text.	Child reading *The ABCs of Plants*: (Pointing to parts of the picture) "The plant is growing from the dirt. The flowers grow from the plant, and they can be yellow or purple . . . Here's the plant coming up out of the ground. My grandpa's plants are this high, like that one" (points to a photograph in the text).

Figure 6.2

 Clip 6.2 *Sebastian Reads* My Football Book *(Informational)*
http://smarturl.it/Clip6.2

In this video, Sebastian is reading a book about football. He's describing the action on the pages and he adds a little bit of dialogue when he imagines what the players in the illustrations might be saying. The important thing to know about Sebastian is that he began this book by reading it in a way characteristic of Level 1, but by the end of the text, he was saying more about the pictures on each page.

Clip 6.3 *Jake Reads* Red-Eyed Tree Frog *(Informational)*

http://smarturl.it/Clip6.3

As we watch Jake read *Red-Eyed Tree Frog*, we hear him elaborate on what he sees in the pictures, even including some editorializing about whether or not snakes eat frogs. As Jake reads, he's beginning to notice the same animal (red-eyed tree frog) from page to page. He offers editorial comments about whether a snake would eat the frog (or do they eat rats?). As he turns the pages, he's linking them together simply by saying, "And then . . ."

INFORMATIONAL BOOK LANGUAGE LEVEL 3

At Language Level 3, children sound like they're reading an informational book because they include some typical informational book characteristics. For example, a child reading a book about tigers at Language Level 2 might read, "The baby tiger is walking with his mommy," whereas a child at Language Level 3 might read the same page like this: "Baby tigers walk with the mother tigers to stay safe and find food." The reader at Language Level 3 begins to generalize the information so that it's not only specific to that particular tiger in that particular book but also so it's applicable to tigers in general. Readers at Language Level 3 understand that informational books tend to teach about the topic in general—in this case, the topic of tigers rather than telling a story of a particular tiger. They bring their schema about the topic to the pages.

Readers also integrate topic-specific language, if they know it, and informational text syntax, if they have been exposed to it, into their reading when they are reaching Language Level 3. They might use words like *male tiger* and *female tiger* instead of *boy tiger* or *girl tiger*. They may look at a photograph and say something like, "Tigers are predators who hunt other animals for food, like antelope and giraffes," rather than something less specific, such as "Tigers chase other animals and eat them, like this thing right here (refers to the antelope) and a giraffe."

Children reading at Language Level 3 bring their schema about the topic into their reading. In other words, they do not just elaborate about what they see on a page to make it sound like an informational text, but they also expound on the topic using what they already know about it. They may or may not be accurate, content-wise, but if you were to close your eyes and simply listen to them read, it would sound more like they are reading an informational book (Figure 6.3).

Clip 6.4 *Kinley Reads* Going to a Horse Farm *(Informational)*
http://smarturl.it/Clip6.4

Kinley reads a book about horses in a way that's characteristic of Language Level 3. She elaborates using a variety of details within the pictures, from colors, to positions, to size. We listen as she changes her syntax from "Horses . . ." to "All horses . . ." to "They are . . . ," and at a point in the text she begins attending to the people in the illustrations and starts her reading on those pages with "Some people . . . ." As she proceeds through the text (around 1:45), she says more and more about the pictures, and her cadence suggests she's trying to sounds like she's reading the words and not naming what's in the pictures.

Informational Book Language Level 3

Description	Sample Transcript
• The child recognizes that this book is teaching about something and may use domain-specific vocabulary. • The child may include his own information about the topic, which may or may not be accurate. • The child may try to say as much as she can think of about the illustrations. • The child may use schema from previous experiences with informational text with regard to how she structures and organizes her reading.	Child reading *The ABCs of Plants*: (Pointing to parts of the picture) "There are lots of different parts of a plant, like the flower, this part (which I forgot), and the leaves and the dirt. I mean the soil. Flowers live in soil and the roots come out in the soil to get food and water for it. The roots can go anywhere and they can get all tangled up sometimes."

Figure 6.3

Conferring About Informational Books with Young Readers

When we sit beside a young child who is reading an informational text, we are likely to support him in one or more of these areas, depending on what we observe the child doing as he turns the pages. We might offer support on how to:

- read with increasing sophistication and intention, in general (i.e., more elaboration, use of domain-specific vocabulary, more attention and consideration to the graphic elements)
- figure out the information on the page or in the graphic element (what's this page/picture teaching me about the topic?)
- read the text so that it sounds like an informational text

To best support children's growing comfort and familiarity with informational books, we can't emphasize enough the importance of providing children with many examples by regularly reading aloud informational books whether or not they connect to a study, inquiry, or theme.

We suggest reading aloud about a variety of topics, including some topics for which the children have a lot of background knowledge and topics for which the children have little or no schema. When we read aloud books about very familiar topics, children hear how authors of informational text present their information. Doing so provides two different scaffolds—our reading provides a model of what it sounds like when someone reads informational text, and the texts provide mentors for how informational texts may go. When children pick up a book about a familiar topic, they can read it by aligning their background knowledge of topic-specific vocabulary and content with the graphic elements on the pages.

On the other hand, when we read aloud texts for which the children don't have much schema at all, we can model how readers look closely at graphic elements to learn new information. Then, when children independently choose an informational text about a topic they don't know much about, they'll be more likely to find their way into and through the text because doing so has been modeled over and over.

We also want to show children a variety of types of informational texts that have different features and purposes. Although teachers, caregivers, and booksellers may tend to lump different types of informational texts into one all-inclusive category, there are different types that serve different purposes: expository, procedural, persuasive, and narrative (Duke et al. 2006/2007).

When we regularly read aloud and talk about a variety of informational books, we provide our children with models and schema for the sound and form of informational texts. Then, when our children have regular opportunities to explore and read informational texts on their own, before they're even reading conventionally, they will use what they know to approach the task of reading informational texts with more intention, confidence, and investment.

When children read informational books independently, we sit beside them and offer support and instruction for a variety of things, including how to read informational texts using the graphic elements, how to integrate their schema and content knowledge into their reading, and how to read in a way that sounds like an informational text.

It's worth mentioning, too, that our conferring default position is always to enjoy the text with the young child. We are willing to join children in playing with texts because our frontline hopes are to facilitate welcoming, joyful interactions with books as they enter the world of reading them.

As you read the following conferring ideas, please know that when we work with young children, our ideas of conferring are more nebulous than they might be for children who are reading conventionally. We aren't trying to make young children jump language levels. Instead, as we sit beside them, we are identifying what they are doing or trying to do and then figuring out the best way to support them or to nudge them forward.

CONFERRING WITH READERS OF INFORMATIONAL BOOK LANGUAGE LEVEL 1

When children read informational books with Language Level 1 characteristics, they are mostly reading in one- or two-word phrases, and they often quickly turn the pages. Also, many young children who are English language learners may read informational texts in Language Level 1 because they might not have the schema or vocabulary to elaborate on the topic or the graphic elements. Our overall goals then, for any reader in Language Level 1, are to support elaboration and thoughtful attention to the graphic elements in the text (Figure 6.4).

CONFERRING WITH READERS AT INFORMATIONAL BOOK LANGUAGE LEVEL 2

Children who read with characteristics of Language Level 2 are often between two worlds. There may be times when they sound more like a Language Level 1, and there may be books that they read with characteristics of Language Level 3. Our typical approach in conferring with these children (or truly, any child) is to build upon what they are already able to do so that they do higher-level work with more consistency. Often for young readers at Language Level 2, we may read a bit of the text to fill in content gaps (Figure 6.5).

Informational Book Language Level 1

Examples of What a Child Might Do While Reading	What Might We Do or Say to Support or Nudge This Child?	Example of an Interaction Between Child and Adult
• Stares at the first pages and does not say anything	• We can let the child know there are lots of ways to read a book. • We can tell the child the title and talk about the cover a bit. • We can give a very quick summary or overview of the text, if we know it. • We can provide language models for how to talk off of a picture.	Child: "I don't know how to read this." Adult: "Well, let's see. It's called *The ABCs of Plants*, and it looks like the kind of book that will teach us stuff about plants. I see some plants, some flowers, and trees right here on the cover." Child: "A girl." Adult: "Yeah, that girl is climbing a tree. Let's look inside and learn some stuff! (goes to the first page) There's a plant, and I see labels that tell us the parts. Plants have a stem" (points to the label near the leaves). Child: "Leafs?" Adult: "Yeah, let's read it: 'Plants have leaves.' What else?" Child: (points to roots) Adult: "Will you read that part?" Child: "Plants have roots?" Adult: "Wow, we just learned the parts of a plant by looking at the picture and saying what we see."
• Names and labels objects with one or two words	• We can ask what the child notices in the pictures to help the child move from one- or two-word labeling to sentences and toward more elaboration. • We can encourage the child to name more things that she sees on the pages. • We can provide language models for full sentences and elaboration. (The prompts are similar to those for Familiar Books Language Level 1.)	Child: (looking at a photograph of a cactus) "That's pointy. Sharp." Adult: "Those are cactus leaves. How can we read that part?" Child: "The cactus leaves?" Adult: "Yeah, and you said they were pointy and sharp. You can read that part too." Child: "The cactus leaves are pointy and sharp?" Adult: "Wow, so you read the picture and you even gave more information about it by describing what it looks like."

Figure 6.4

Informational Book Language Level 1 (Continued)

Examples of What a Child Might Do While Reading	What Might We Do or Say to Support or Nudge This Child?	Example of an Interaction Between Child and Adult
• May not connect one page to another	• We can help the child connect his thinking from one page to the next. • We can model how to bring random ideas back to the text.	Child: "The baby plant. (turns page) Trees. (turns page) I forgot what that's called." Adult: "That kind of plant is called a cactus. You know, this whole book is about plants, so should we try to read it that way? Here's what I mean: (reads title) '*The ABCs of Plants*' (turns to first page). 'Some plants can be baby plants. Some plants can be trees.' Your turn" (turns page). Child: "Some plants are um …" Adult: "Cactus plants." Child: "Some plants are cactus plants."

Figure 6.4 (Continued)

Informational Book Language Level 2

Examples of What a Child Might Do While Reading	What Might We Do or Say to Support or Nudge This Child?	Example of an Interaction Between Child and Adult
• Attends to pictures and illustrations and names and labels objects with more elaboration	• We can teach the child to use both the observations of the details in the pictures as well as the content knowledge the child has about the topic to read with more elaboration.	Child: "Cactuses are really pointy and they have sharp prickers. It would hurt if you touched it." Adult: "Wanna know something else about the prickly parts? It says here that the prickly leaves keep the animals from eating it." Child: "Yeah, it would hurt the animal's mouth if he ate that. Nom. Nom. Nom *ouch*!" (laughs). Adult: "That *would* hurt. Yikes. Let's try to read this part using our new information. I'll start by reading what you said the first time: Cactuses are really pointy and they have sharp prickers." Child: "The prickers are good for keeping animals away so they don't eat them." Adult: "OK. You know what? Next time you read this, make sure you read *all* that juicy information. Cactuses are really pointy and they have sharp prickers. The prickers are good because they keep animals from eating them." *Continues*

Figure 6.5

Informational Book Language Level 2 (Continued)

Examples of What a Child Might Do While Reading	What Might We Do or Say to Support or Nudge This Child?	Example of an Interaction Between Child and Adult
• At times, tries to read the text in a way that sounds like he's putting the information into a more cohesive whole	• We can teach the child some ways to make "topic sentences" for a page (without calling them that). • We can teach the child to use specific language (or we can teach the vocabulary) so that it sounds "official."	Child: "There are plants in the forest and there are plants in the water." Adult: "You know what that place is called? It's called a *wetland*." Child: "A wetland?" Adult: "Yes. So you said just read that plants grow in forests and plants in grow in wetlands. Let's think about this. It's all about the places plants can grow. Let's see. Plants can grow in lots of places, like ..." (hands it off to child). Child: "Plants can grow in lots of places like the forest or the wetlands." Adult: "That sounded *just* like an informational text because you used the expert word, *wetland*, and you put the information together."
• Does not reveal any informational text schema (The child labels the pages because he doesn't know much about the topic.)	• We can remind the child that this book is teaching about something by saying, "What does this picture teach you about *X*?" • We can teach the child to look at a graphic element and say, "This is teaching me that ..." or "This is showing me that ..."	Child: "The sun and the plant ..." (turns page). Adult: "Ooh, wait a moment. Let's read this page together. You said, 'the sun and the plant.' But let's try to read the information in this picture." Child: "I don't know about it." Adult: "Well, let's see if the picture can help us figure some stuff out. What do we see? What is this picture showing us? The sun is shining on the plant ..." Child: "There's water here." Adult: "The sun shines on the plant and the water ..." Child: "The plants needs it. Adult: "The sun shines on the plant and the water feeds the plant ... Is anything else this picture is teaching us?" Child: "The dirt?" Adult: "Oh, right, that's soil. Have you heard that word? *Soil*? It's another word for *dirt*." Child: "Soil is for the plant too." Adult: "OK. So we've got the sun and the water and the soil. So let's see if we can read this picture ..." Child: "The plant has the sun and the water and the soil." Adult: "See what happened? We looked really closely at this picture and thought about what it was showing us and that helped us read it."

Figure 6.5 (Continued)

Informational Book Language Level 2 (Continued)

Examples of What a Child Might Do While Reading	What Might We Do or Say to Support or Nudge This Child?	Example of an Interaction Between Child and Adult
• May switch between reading the text and editorializing as she reads	• We can gently direct the editorializing toward content-based comments. • We can also enjoy the editorializing and have a conversation about that.	Child: "My grandma has a thing like this, and I pricked my finger on it because these are so sharp. It hurt, and I didn't like this kind." Adult: "Are you telling me your grandma has a cactus plant in her house?" Child: "Yeah, and it's so sharp and prickery." Adult: "The prickers are like the leaves for a cactus" (paraphrasing from the actual text). Child: "My grandma says that they're in the desert and I saw them in *Rango*, too." Adult: "Yeah, there are lots of kinds of cactuses, or cacti, some people say, and they live in dry places like deserts." Child: "I don't want those kind. *Ow!* They hurt." Adult: "What's with the prickers, anyway? Why prickers for leaves?" Child: "They hurt people, so people won't take them."
• Sounds like he is reading a story about the topic rather than conveying information; he doesn't yet sound like he is reading an expository informational text	• We can nudge the child toward making his reading sound expository. • We can model and share the language and syntax of expository informational text.	Child: "Cactuses are so prickly and their prickers can hurt. Ouch, it hurts! Ouch, ouch, ouch! (touching the photographs of the various cacti) Oh, look this one has flowers and prickers." Adult: "Wow, let's see here. You said cacti have prickers and flowers. What else?" Child: "They have prickers and flowers, and uh . . . I don't know." Adult: "Let's look at the pictures and see what they might teach us. Let's see, cacti have prickers and flowers. They can be tall and skinny . . ." (points to another picture). Child: "They can be round and small like a ball or something." Adult: "Wow, we sound like we're reading information. Wanna say it like we're teaching the stuff from this page?" Child: (nods) Adult: "I'll start. Cacti have prickers and . . ." Child: "Flowers." Adult: "And they can be . . ." (points to the tall cactus). Child: "Tall or round like a ball."

Figure 6.5 (Continued)

Mary Alice Berry is conferring with Griffon, a kindergarten student who is reading a book about butterflies. He has learned that one way to read an information book is to imagine you're the object on the page and tell about yourself by looking closely at the pictures and describing what you see and what it teaches you about the object. At first, the child is reading the text with a simple, patterned approach. He reads the early pages with a "I am a butterfly. I can fly," sort of pattern. At one point, he gets stuck because he's not sure what the bug is on the page, so Mary Alice suggests that instead of being something specific, if he didn't know, he could read it, "I am a bug. I can . . . ." In this instance, Mary Alice is offering an on-the-run idea to help the child deal with difficulty.

As he reads on, Mary Alice stops him to make a teaching point that will help grow his work. She names the strong work he's doing before she teaches him a strategy that will help him say more about what's on each page. She suggests he look closely at the pictures and say what he sees in more detail. Before sending him to do this on his own, Mary Alice models it for him. As you watch, the child easily takes this strategy and uses it as he moves forward in the text. This suggests that Mary Alice found the sweet spot in this interaction. Whenever we teach something that is new that a child is able to do we've met them right where they are and moved them to new or deeper work.

CONFERRING WITH READERS OF INFORMATIONAL BOOK LANGUAGE LEVEL 3

Children who read informational texts with characteristics of Language Level 3 have often heard informational text read aloud to them, and this is reflected in the syntax they use as they read. Some ways we can support readers at this level are to help them build content knowledge and domain-specific vocabulary, to teach them ways to read various graphic elements, and to show them how one book on a topic can lead to another (Figure 6.6).

Anytime we confer with children, whether they're writing little books, reading texts, building a block structure, making art, or anything else, we watch closely. Yet when we watch, it's as if we're watching several facets of the child at once. We're watching their attitudes; we're looking for signs of engagement; we're noticing their use of strategies; we're attending to their language use; and so on. We're figuring out how to best help this child move from one place as a learner to another. And sometimes the most important move we can help them make is the move from "I can't do it" to "I did it."

Informational Book Language Level 3

Examples of What a Child Might Do While Reading	What Might We Do or Say to Support or Nudge This Child?	Example of an Interaction Between Child and Adult
• Recognizes that this book is teaching about something and may use vocabulary specific to the topic	• We can help the child learn more content by reading bits or by directing the child toward text features.	Child: "Plants can grow in deserts where it's really hot." Adult: "Yeah, that's how I read this too. Oh, look, there are some labels. What's labeled here? I see a tree … a bush …" Child: "Flowers …" Adult: "I think it's also teaching us about what kinds of desert plants grow, too. You read, 'Plants can grow in deserts where it's really hot. For example, trees can grow …'" Child: "'Flowers can grow …'" Adult: "'And bushes can grow.' See how we did that? We read the page and noticed the labels that tell us that there's more information we can include."
• May include his own information about the topic in a way that may or may not be accurate	• We can search the text for features that may lead the child to revise his misconceptions.	Child: "Some plants are cactuses and they have these really sharp prickers. They shoot the prickers out to kill other plants and other animals. Bew Bew Bew Bew" (shooting sound). Adult: "Huh? Where'd you learn that? I've never heard that before." Child: "The prickers are sharp like those things, like um, those things like arrows, and they shoot off them to kill stuff." Adult: "Is something you learned or is it something that you're thinking because the prickers remind you of arrows?" Child: (shrugs) Adult: "Well, let's see here, it says that the prickly leaves help to protect the plant from animals who want to eat it." Child: "Yeah, because the animals can't eat the prickers." Adult: "So what are you thinking now?" Child: "The prickers are sharp so animals won't eat them." Adult: "What about the cactus shooting the prickers like arrows? Bew Bew?" Child: (smiles) Adult: "That would be a cartoon cactus—like a superhero cactus. I'm *Super Cactus*—Bew Bew. Not a real cactus."

Continues

Figure 6.6

Informational Book Language Level 3 (Continued)

Examples of What a Child Might Do While Reading	What Might We Do or Say to Support or Nudge This Child?	Example of an Interaction Between Child and Adult
• May use schema from previous experiences with informational text with regard to how she structures and organizes her reading	• We can support the child with more specialized vocabulary about the topic. • We can teach the child how to read various graphic elements (by *read*, we don't necessarily mean conventionally).	Child: "This is the plant. It grows from a seed." Adult: "Ooh, look—it's a life cycle. See these arrows. We can read it and use these arrows to tell the story of the information. I'll start here (I usually start at the top). The plant starts out as a seed, and then..." Child: "Then someone plants it so it becomes a little plant." Adult: "And then..." Child: "It grows into a flower or a big plant." Adult: "You just read this diagram of the plant's life cycle. If you see another one of these in other books, you can do what we just did. Start from the top, and follow the arrows around, telling the information of the pictures at each arrow. You know, I just realized that books about insects often have these too."

Figure 6.6 (Continued)

Growing Independence with Text

W e wait for children to reach independence milestones that may seem unimaginable at a particular point in time. The parent of a colicky infant may not be able to imagine a quiet, uneventful, straight-to-sleep bedtime. A mom who feels her toddler cling tightly to her leg as they walk into a birthday party struggles to envision her hesitant child getting on a school bus by herself someday. A dad who prods, reminds, and cajoles his middle school child to handle his chores may find it hard to believe his son will be a responsible housemate in college. The parents of a high school student who is constantly negotiating delicate social situations may find it inconceivable that their fickle teenager will someday be ready or willing to have a long-term relationship.

When we're waiting, it can seem like all the other children of the same age have reached these independence milestones already. The mothers in our baby group share success stories about smooth bedtime routines. Everyone else's child runs with abandon into the birthday party. Our neighbor's son looks happy when he's mowing the lawn, and our teenage niece lives a drama-free high school life. Yet, we hold on to hope that the time will eventually come when our baby falls asleep on his own, when our little girl gets on the school bus with a smile, when our son takes care of his chores without any nagging to do so. We know there will be a day when our daughter settles down, ready and able to deal with the challenges of being in a long-term partnership.

Here's the thing: there is no official date that these independence milestones occur, nor do they occur at the same age (or at all) for everyone. That's the thing about independence milestones—there's a fierce independence about them. They vary from person to person, and their timing depends on so many different factors and inputs.

This is certainly the case for children in early childhood classrooms, rigid standards and grade-level expectations notwithstanding. Ask kindergarten teachers about the first day of school, whether that first day is in Newark, New Jersey, or Billings, Montana. Some children saunter into the classroom on day one as if they owned the place, and others spend their first day intermittently sobbing for their moms. Eventually, all of the children will be used to the routines of the classroom and the separation from their families, but it doesn't happen for all children at the same time.

Children's academic independence varies along a continuum where one end is "No, I can't" and the other end is "I can do it myself." For example, in preschool classrooms many teachers ask children to sign in each day. For some children, that brings a level of stress and worry, and they may need a nurturing adult to help them for a period of time, but other children scribble lines and curly cues and consider themselves signed in and ready to face what the day has to offer. Still others walk in on day one and sign in without even being asked. They simply saw other children doing it, so they did it, too, without prompting. Teachers realize that children's willingness to independently take on the task of writing their names to sign in doesn't always correlate with their abilities to write their name conventionally. We've watched children who do know how to spell and form the letters of their name get teary eyed when asked to do so, whereas children who don't know all the letters of their name are eager to sign in with what they do know.

We want children to take on the task of reading anything, with or without an adult nearby, and to achieve this, we need to explicitly support and teach into their growing independence.

When we look across the year at all our instructional and environmental priorities in early childhood classrooms—from socialization to communication, from literacy to numeracy, from gross motor to fine motor skills, and so on—it may seem that independence is implicitly taught and supported within all of these domains. That may be true, but for many children, implicit instruction is invisible instruction. Some children may need very explicit strategies for how to initiate and how to maintain their work and play on their own.

With regard to reading texts before reading texts conventionally, we've realized that it's important to support children's independence with the task itself, in addition to nudging their language levels and nurturing their meaning-making skills. We want children to take on the task of reading anything, with or without an adult nearby, and to achieve this, we need to explicitly support and teach into their growing independence.

Independence Levels

As we watch young children read texts before they can read conventionally, we see a range of willingness, a variety of stalling strategies, and a lot of attitude shifts. Some children seek frequent adult assurances and ask for help and others jump right in and read the book as if the adult wasn't even there. Some children's independence levels change quickly and grow within one book, but others remain hesitant across books.

This wasn't a surprise because we know that children present a variety of independence levels on tasks throughout the day. What was surprising, however, was that we learned that it's relatively easy to nudge a child's sense of agency from "I can't read" to "I can read this myself."

Clip 7.1 *Alice Reads* Hello Twins *(Unfamiliar)*
http://smarturl.it/Clip7.1

Alice is a three-year-old who is already aware that there is a "right" way to read. When Matt asks her if she would read a text to him, she begins by saying, "I don't really know how to read." Then they begin to volley back and forth. When Matt asks what she does when she has a book, Alice says she reads books by "looking at it like that," referring to turning the pages and looking at the pictures. Then Matt gives her a quick strategy for looking at the pictures and telling what she sees. She gently rebuffs this nudge by saying, "I can just read in my mind." So, again, Matt returns her volley by saying that if she reads in her mind, then he wouldn't get to hear it. At that point, he models how to tell what she sees in the picture. Matt then gives her the chance to do the same, and when she continues to hesitate, Matt prompts and nudges her as they turn the pages together. He does this for a few minutes as they read this book. Alice never really takes on the task by herself in this text, and Matt doesn't force her to do so. He remains her partner in this endeavor rather than her taskmaster.

At the end, Matt wraps up with Alice by recognizing how she changed from the start of the book to the end. Alice acknowledges that she said she couldn't read it at first, but then she did read the book by looking at the pictures. A surprising thing happens next. As Matt and another child read in the background, Alice takes a book on her own and does all the things Matt showed her when they were reading together. She does this by herself. Without the nudges and the support of the conference with Matt, Alice would have likely continued to look at books the way she said she did at first, turning the pages and reading, as she said, "in her head," but with this little conference that contained strategy support and explicit naming of her growth, Alice very quickly became more independent and more intentional.

INDEPENDENCE LEVELS WHILE READING FAMILIAR, UNFAMILIAR, AND INFORMATIONAL TEXTS

Children's independence levels with the task of reading a text before they can read conventionally vary. Similar to the way the language approaches children used when reading helped us see levels of sophistication, we were able to observe some trends in children's willingness and abilities to take on the task independently. We categorized these trends into three levels.

Independence Level 1

At Independence Level 1, children are hesitant or reluctant and they frequently appeal to the teacher or the parent for assurance, guidance, or direction (Figure 7.1). They need an adult to support them all the way through the book. If the adult gives a pointer or a suggestion for how to read the book on one's own, the child may use the strategy immediately, but then he may need support again when he turns to a new page. The child reading at Independence Level 1 needs ongoing support in order to continue reading.

We invite you to look again at the video clip of Alice because she exhibits the characteristics, in that particular book, of a child who reads with an Independence Level 1 approach. The important words in this case are "in that particular book" because Alice quickly changes to a higher level of independence in the next book she chooses.

Independence Level 2

When a child is showing characteristics of Independence Level 2, he may need some prompting, encouragement, or assurance from an adult to get going at the beginning of the book, but after a couple of pages the child reads on his own (Figure 7.2). He may still

Independence Level 1

Description	Conferring Support We Can Offer
• The child may begin by saying, "I can't read," or "I don't know the words." • The child looks at the adult frequently. • The child needs a prompt or nudge on almost every page. • The child is easily distracted. • The child relies mostly on the adult to support her reading and doesn't independently access the pictures, her schema for the story, or her content knowledge to read on her own.	• If children are concerned because they can't read conventionally, we can reassure them by letting them know there's a way to read that involves reading the pictures and illustrations. • We can use the rhythm of, "Watch me. Now you try," as we move through the interaction. • We can name what they did and show them how they changed throughout the book—"At first you said you couldn't read it, but then you were reading every page because you looked so closely at the pictures." • We can teach for transfer by saying things like, "So now that you've read this one, which book do you want to read next?"

Figure 7.1

Independence Level 2

Description	Conferring Support We Can Offer
• The child may begin by saying, "I can't read," or "I don't know the words." • The child needs a prompt or nudge at the beginning of the book but quickly takes over after a page or two. • The child may talk to the adult or ask questions but he is not appealing for help. • The child relies mostly on the pictures, story schema, or content knowledge to support her reading.	• If children are concerned because they can't read conventionally, we can reassure them by letting them know there's a way to read that involves reading the pictures and illustrations. • For the first page or two (or three) we can use the rhythm of, "Watch me. You try," as we move through the text. At a point soon after, we can say, "Now you read it. I can tell you're ready!" • We can acknowledge what they did to read so that it can be transferred to another book. "Wow, you're giving these characters some words. That's a great way you can read a book" or "I notice that you're telling about what's going on in the pictures. You're reading the pictures. Keep going!"

Figure 7.2

stop from time to time and ask an adult a question or talk about what he sees on the page, but he doesn't *need* the adult to be able to continue. The interaction between the adult and the child can be characterized as mostly conversational after the adult provides the initial boost into the book.

Independence Level 3

When children read at Independence Level 3, they do not appeal for help at all (Figure 7.3). They read the book independently and would do so even if an adult isn't sitting beside them or asking them to read. If an adult is there, they may talk about the book, but the interaction between the child and the book is primary, and any interactions with the adult are secondary.

Clip 7.2 *Natasha Reads* Hello Twins *(Unfamiliar)*
http://smarturl.it/Clip7.2

Natasha willingly takes on the task of reading the text *Hello Twins*. Right away, she zooms in and tells the story of the pictures by giving the characters dialogue, and as she turns the pages, she elaborates, using the details. Natasha does a variety of things as she reads, from describing the actions on the pages to giving voice to the characters in the story. Matt chimes in here and there but not out of necessity. Natasha does not appeal for help. Instead, Matt is positioning himself as her partner, talking about what she

Independence Level 3

Description	Conferring Support We Can Offer
• The child reads with or without an adult present. • The child does not need prompts or nudges as she reads. • The child relies on the pictures and illustrations, story schema, and/or content knowledge. • The child's reading sounds invested and engaged. • The child might ask an adult a question about the content on a page, but once she gets an answer, she'll continue to read on her own.	• We can join the child as a partner, enhancing or echoing what the child is doing. • We can engage the child in meaning-making conversation about the book.

Figure 7.3

sees on the pages, and encouraging her to say more and extend her thinking. It's easy to imagine that if Matt were to move on to another child, Natasha would easily and willingly continue reading this text on her own.

VARIABILITY OF INDEPENDENCE

As we noted in the beginning of this chapter, there are so many factors that affect a child's ability and willingness to do something with independence. In the case of reading a text before they can read conventionally, the variables that surround independence are many, as are the remedies when the child is not approaching the task independently (Figure 7.4).

We also realize that a child's independence level can change quickly. Back in Chapter 3 we saw how Jazzalynn's language level changes and grows from the beginning of the book to the end of a book. If we rewatch Jazzalynn read *Clip-Clop* we can see a similar change in her independence.

Clip 7.3 *Jazzalynn Reads Clip-Clop (Unfamiliar)*

http://smarturl.it/Clip7.3

Variable or Obstacle to Independence	Potential Remedy for Growing Independence
The child is not interested in the text.	• Let the child choose the text.
The child is not familiar with the text and is hesitant.	• Start with a familiar text and then move to an unfamiliar one.
The child is concerned about reading the text "the right way."	• Assure the child that there are different ways to read a book when you're three/four/five/six/seven.
The child is having an off day for whatever reason—she might be worried about something, moody, not feeling well, tired, or so on.	• Assess the situation and decide in favor of maintaining as positive an interaction with the text as possible, especially if the child is unusually hesitant or reluctant.

Figure 7.4

On the first page, Matt helps Jazzalynn figure out what to say by asking her questions about what she sees on the page. Matt also prompts her to turn the page and keep going. But just several minutes later Jazzalynn is turning pages and reading independently. Her interactions with Matt are now based on engagement and conversation about the book, rather than one of dependence where Jazzalynn needs Matt to be able to continue.

The Intersection Between the Language Levels and the Independence Levels

Anytime we confer with young children about their work, we're faced with many possibilities for what we might support, nudge, or teach the child. We often suggest applying the emergency room principle—attend to the chest pains before the sprained ankle. In other words, we try to triage the child's needs and attend to what seems most pressing or integral to her development, engagement level, and intentions.

Consider for a moment a conference with Sydney, a pre-K writer. One day in mid-November, she chose to go the bookmaking center, which was a surprise to Tamara, her teacher. Sydney rarely ever self-initiated any writing, and when she had a choice, she would choose most anything else.

Anyway, on this particular day, Sydney took a little blank book from the paper supply tray and began to illustrate it. Tamara sat down beside her and watched for a moment. Sydney had illustrated the first couple of pages with what looked like animals. But she stopped abruptly and looked at her teacher. "What are you thinking about?" Tamara asked.

"I'm done," Sydney said as she stood up and started putting the markers back into the basket.

In this moment, Tamara had many choices for how to angle her conference. She could work with Sydney on labeling her illustrations with words. She might support Sydney in adding more details to her illustrations. She might ask Sydney to read the book to her and then nudge her to add more pages. She could talk with Sydney about what kind of book she was making and find a mentor text to inspire her to go further. There are many other possibilities.

But when a teacher triages the needs in a conference, perhaps Sydney's greatest needs at that time were to develop the identity of a writer, to believe that she can write books, and to grow independence around the task. When Tamara thought about that moment in time, she remembered that Sydney stopped writing as soon as Tamara sat down. Taking this into consideration along with all she knows about Sydney, including her lukewarm (at best) relationship to writing, Tamara chose to confer with Sydney about her intentions and the possibilities of the book she started and encouraged her to keep going based on what she had said. Tamara chose to have this conference rather than one reminding her about writing words on the pages, even though that was a tempting teaching point because the lack of words on her page was so obvious and public.

Even though it was tempting to work with Sydney on writing words, Tamara realized that the more pressing issue was Sydney's ongoing lack of intention, writing stamina, and engagement.

Similarly, when we work with young readers who are not yet reading conventionally, our conferences might very well be about supporting their independence and intentions so that they are more likely to put themselves into reading situations in which they'll use the reading strategies that we've taught. In other words, every time we sit beside a child, we try to calibrate our conferences so that we nudge him in ways that he can transfer to any other texts, so that he's more inclined to want to read something familiar, unfamiliar, or informational, whether or not he's in the presence or acting on the directive of an adult.

We've found it helpful to overlay the Language Levels with the Independence Levels because this view offers us a rough estimate of the best support to offer a child, the kind of support that will teach her things she didn't realize she could do and show her things she can do on her own, when it's just her and her books.

In Figures 7.5 through 7.10, we share our Independence and Language Level grids, which you will also find in Appendix C. Our hope for all children is that they'll have experiences during which they're reading at a high level of independence as well as a sophisticated language level. We recognize that the place on this grid where a child might be identified is dependent on so many factors—the text, his expressive language abilities, his knowledge of the target language, his awareness of ways to access texts when he doesn't know the words, his intentions, his moods, and so on. And the other confounding factor is that one child can read different texts with very different language levels or independence levels. That's why it's absolutely vital that although we bring the schema of the child and teaching intention into any conference, we still always observe and meet the child in the sweet spot between where she is in that moment and what might be next for that child.

> . . . *every time we sit beside a child, we try to calibrate our conferences so that we nudge him in ways that he can transfer to any other texts, so that he's more inclined to want to read something familiar, unfamiliar, or informational, whether or not he's in the presence or acting on the directive of an adult.*

Language Levels with Familiar Books

Language Level 1	Language Level 2	Language Level 3	Language Level 4
The child • may or may not express familiarity with the text • attends to pictures and illustrations, and may make editorial comments on them, unrelated to the story • names and labels objects and actions from page to page • may not connect one page to another • may not rely on prior exposure to the text • may not attempt to read with accuracy based on prior exposure	**The child** • expresses familiarity • attends to pictures and illustrations • names objects and actions with more detail • connects one page to another to create a cohesive reading • relies on prior exposure to the text to read in a way that's more accurate content-wise to the text	**The child** • expresses high levels of familiarity • attends to pictures and illustrations • names objects and actions with more text-based detail and story language • connects one page to another to create a cohesive reading • relies on prior exposure to the text to read in a way that's more accurate content-wise and language-wise to the text	**The child** • expresses high level of familiarity • relies on prior exposure to the text to read with accurate meaning • attends to pictures and illustrations • connects one page to another to create a cohesive reading • reads aloud with accuracy, using words, phrases, and syntax of the text • reads with intonation and expression

Figure 7.5

Independence Levels with Familiar Books

Independence Level 1	Independence Level 2	Independence Level 3
The child • may begin by saying, "I can't read" or "I don't know the words" • frequently looks to an adult for help • needs a prompt or nudge on almost every page • is easily distracted • doesn't independently access the pictures, her schema for the story, or her content knowledge to read on her own	**The child** • begins by saying, "I can't read," or "I don't know the words" • needs a prompt or nudge at the beginning of the book but quickly takes over after a page or two • may talk to the adult or to ask questions about the text but is not appealing for help • relies mostly on the pictures, story schema, or content knowledge to support her reading	**The child** • reads with or without an adult present • does not need prompts or nudges as she reads • relies on the pictures and illustrations, story schema, and/or content knowledge • sounds invested and engaged • may ask an adult a question about the content on a page, but once she gets an answer, she'll continue to read on her own

Figure 7.6

Language Levels When Reading Unfamiliar Books

Language Level 1	Language Level 2	Language Level 3
The child • attends to pictures and illustrations • names and labels objects without elaboration • may not connect one page to another	**The child** • attends to pictures and illustrations • names and labels objects elaboration and details • tries to connect one page to the next using words like **and** or **and then** • infers characters' feelings and text events that aren't on the page • might imagine character dialogue	**The child** • attends to pictures and illustrations • elaborates more on each page; it sounds like he's reading sentences per page, instead of one line per page • uses text sense and literary language to connect one page to another • infers characters' feelings and text events that aren't on the page • imagines what characters might say • editorializes about the text

Figure 7.7

Independence Levels When Reading Unfamiliar Books

Independence Level 1	Independence Level 2	Independence Level 3
The child • may begin by saying, "I can't read" or "I don't know the words" • frequently looks to an adult for help • needs a prompt or nudge on almost every page • is easily distracted • doesn't independently access the pictures, her schema for the story, or her content knowledge to read on her own	**The child** • begins by saying, "I can't read" or "I don't know the words" • needs a prompt or nudge at the beginning of the book, but quickly takes over after a page or two • may talk to the adult or to ask questions about the text but is not appealing for help • relies mostly on the pictures, story schema, or content knowledge to support her reading	**The child** • reads with or without an adult present • does not need prompts or nudges as she reads • relies on the pictures and illustrations, story schema, and/or content knowledge • sounds invested and engaged • may ask an adult a question about the content on a page, but once she gets an answer, she'll continue to read on her own

Figure 7.8

Language Levels Levels When Reading Informational Books

Language Level 1	Language Level 2	Language Level 3
The child • attends to pictures and illustrations • names and labels objects without elaboration • may not connect one page to another • may not reveal any schema for how informational texts tend to go	**The child** • attends to pictures and illustrations • names and labels objects with more elaboration • tries to read the text in a way that sounds like he's putting the information into a more cohesive whole • may switch between reading the text and editorializing as she reads • sounds like he is reading a story about the topic rather than conveying information; he doesn't yet sound like he is reading an informational book	**The child** • recognizes that this book is teaching about something and may use domain-specific vocabulary • includes his own information about the topic, which may or may not be accurate • may try to say as much as she can think of about the illustrations • may use schema from previous experiences with how informational text might sound and reflect this in how she structures and organizes her reading

Figure 7.9

Independence Levels When Reading Informational Books

Independence Level 1	Independence Level 2	Independence Level 3
The child • may begin by saying, "I can't read" or "I don't know the words" • frequently looks to an adult for help • needs a prompt or nudge on almost every page • is easily distracted • doesn't independently access the pictures, her schema for the story, or her content knowledge to read on her own	**The child** • begins by saying, "I can't read" or "I don't know the words" • needs a prompt or nudge at the beginning of the book but quickly takes over after a page or two • may talk to the adult or ask questions about the text but is not appealing for help • relies mostly on the pictures, story schema, or content knowledge to support her reading	**The child** • reads with or without an adult present • does not need prompts or nudges as she reads • relies on the pictures and illustrations, story schema, and/or content knowledge • sounds invested and engaged • may ask an adult a question about the content on a page, but once she gets an answer, she'll continue to read on her own

Figure 7.10

CHAPTER 8

Supporting Preschool Readers Before They're Reading Conventionally

One morning, Mary looked around her preschool classroom and paused for a moment to savor the buzz of engagement. Two children were in the block area trying to figure out ways to connect their block towers without knocking anything over. A half-dozen little sculptors were at the art table kneading and rolling clay into snakes and other animal shapes. Three kids were making books at the round table near the front of the room, and a couple of children were working with the classroom assistant to get snacks ready for the others.

Meanwhile, the library corner was bustling with kids leaning into each other as they looked through books together. It was there that Mary noticed Dequan. He was sitting near some other children reading a book about dinosaurs by himself. Dequan was passionate about the topic, and he was the resident dinosaur expert. He not only knew the names of the A-list dinosaurs, but he could identify some of the more obscure ones.

Mary sat beside Dequan and asked, "Would you read this book to me?" Mary regularly asked children to read to her, so Dequan was comfortable with this request. Although he wasn't decoding the words yet, he had developed a healthy image of himself as a reader because even at an early age, he had regular and authentic opportunities to assume that identity.

So Dequan turned back to the first page of his dinosaur book and started reading it aloud. On the page where he saw a dinosaur standing, he said, "Sauropods are big. They have big feet." On the page where a dinosaur was eating ferns, Dequan said, "They can eat plants. I forgot what that's called."

Mary said, "The plant or the dinosaur?"

"When they eat plants. What's that called?" Dequan asked.

"Oh, do you mean *herbivore*—the kind of dinosaur that eats plants?"

"Yeah, this dinosaur is a herbivore 'cause he's eating plants. He's a stegosaurus," Dequan said, returning to the page.

This is how it went. Dequan would turn the pages and read the pictures by telling what he saw in them, and then he would chat with Mary to ask questions or talk about cool information. The tone of their interaction was warm and conversational and it lasted no more than three minutes. After a few pages, Mary left Dequan to observe and support other children in the classroom. When it was time to get ready for recess, Dequan was still reading the dinosaur book aloud, in much the same way he had been reading it to Mary. Two other children had moved over to listen to him.

Mary's interaction with Dequan, asking him to read to her, was typical for this preschool class. Dequan and his classmates are used to reading to adults, although they weren't earlier in the year. As this year progressed, reading aloud to their teacher and to each other (even though most weren't yet reading conventionally) had become as natural for the children as building with blocks or painting at the easel or running at recess.

Here's the thing. This can happen in any preschool class because the conditions that allow it to happen are simple and replicable: books, time, and expectations that children can and want to read before they can figure out the words. Dequan and his classmates' images of themselves as readers have been intentionally nurtured and fostered every day, and so it's actually unremarkable to Mary that Dequan read her the dinosaur book. After all, he and his classmates have been doing this almost all year largely because Mary has asked a simple question, "Would you read this book to me?"

In our travels, we always ask preschool teachers how often they ask a child (who isn't yet decoding) to read a book to them while listening to what the child is doing. Most teachers say that they don't ask children to read to them regardless of whether they are holding a familiar book, an unfamiliar book, or an informational book, whether it's familiar or unfamiliar.

The reasons for this are well intentioned. First, many early childhood educators strive to protect the integrity of a child's preschool experience. Preschool should not be like kindergarten or first grade, they say. We agree wholeheartedly. That's why the reading experiences we support in preschool classrooms are invitational, not assigned. Reading in pre-K starts with the child. It is about helping children to develop confident identities as readers and a comfort with all kinds of texts; the daily work and play of pre-K is not about getting children ready for some high-stakes test they'll take down the road.

We share concern about the constant pressure to accelerate learning and the increased academic intensity of pre-K curricula. We're concerned that teachers are pushed to drill and test our youngest children in the name of college and career readiness. We're concerned that recess and play have given way to rigor and rubrics. We don't want to feed into this mind-set with this book. After all, as we wrote in the introduction, if we do what's right for young children by meeting them where they are as learners and nurturing them from there, readiness will be the by-product. It doesn't have to be the primary goal in our interactions with young children.

> *Our goal for all young children is that they have an image of themselves as readers, whether or not they can read the words yet.*

Another reason that preschool teachers may not typically ask their children to read is that they might believe that children need to have some sound–symbol knowledge and be able to recognize a few high-frequency words before they are ready. This is true only if we limit the definition of reading to be the act of "reading the words." If, on the other hand, we believe that reading also includes the vital act of making meaning, and if we believe that young readers can read pictures, then we can more easily imagine sitting beside a four-year-old who has *Olivia Saves the Circus* on her lap and saying to her, "Ooh, I love Olivia books. Would you read this one to me?"

In this chapter we want to provide a vision for how we might support preschool readers (keeping in mind that these children are three, four, and five years old) to develop identities as readers, as people who are able and willing to interact with any text with strategies that meet children where they are. Our goal for all young children is that they have an image of themselves as readers, whether or not they can read the words yet.

Beliefs That Frame Our Reading Work with Pre-K Children

We begin by sharing some beliefs because these infuse everything we do—how we set up the classroom environment, how we structure our day, how we interact with children, and what expectations we hold for children's growth.

- We believe that it's important to have a wide variety of books in preschool classrooms, including familiar, unfamiliar, and informational books, as well as other genres, like ABC books, wordless books, concept books, and so on. It's helpful to have a space for a classroom library, with baskets of books on bookshelves that are easily accessible to children. It sends a powerful message to have books available all around the room as well, because we want children to know that they can read about anything and that books go right along with any of their interests.

For example, near the class fish tank, there might be a basket of texts, including books about different kinds of fish and books about taking care of fish. The basket might also contain an aquarium supply catalog, a copy of *Swimmy* by Leo Lionni, a laminated brochure of types of fish, and so on. The block area might contain a basket with how-to books about building or architecture books that featuring different types of structures. There may be postcards of iconic buildings. The art area might have a selection of kids' art books, artists' biographies, pages from old art calendars, texts sets for artist studies or art "genre" studies and so on.

- We believe in an expansive vision of what it means to be a reader. We want children to know that there are three-, four-, and five-year-old ways to read and that a person can read a book before she can read the words. We'll support children with developing visual literacy by looking at and talking about pictures and illustrations that are inside and outside texts, such as works of art. Similar to the way children are writers even before they can write words conventionally because they can compose and communicate on paper, we want to send a clear message that children can be readers, even before they read the words on a page because they can look closely at texts to make meaning and express their thoughts about them.

- We believe there are many points of entry to conventional reading. We support children on their journey to conventional reading in pre-K by giving them lots of time and opportunity to write and to play with literacy across the day.

- We believe in the importance and effectiveness of focusing on comprehension and meaning making before and while we focus on decoding. Supporting children to decode proficiently and comprehend deeply are part of the ultimate goal, but we don't view decoding as a prerequisite for comprehension, at any age.

- We believe students need regular reading interactions with adults, including adults reading *to* children, adults reading *with* children, children reading *to* adults, and children reading *with* and *to* each other.

- We believe we can best support young children when we watch them closely and when our support begins with what they can do already, regardless of their age.

We want to guard against the default position of simply lifting a version of a kindergarten reading workshop and miniaturizing it for preschool classroom. Although the underlying beliefs for preschool and kindergarten may be largely the same, we believe the structures, materials, and expectations that work well and are appropriate for kindergarten are different from what we'd recommend for prekindergarten classrooms.

A Day in the Life of a Preschool Classroom

In this section, we'll share ideas for how to structure parts of the school day to best nurture preschool children's relationships to books and to develop their healthy identity as readers.

We're committed workshop teachers. Most of our work lives are devoted to helping elementary school teachers implement joyful, intentional, and effective reading and writing workshops, yet we do not envision a formal or structured reading workshop, characterized by a whole-class minilesson, reading time, and share time, in preschool classrooms.

First, whole-group reading instruction followed by simultaneous independent reading time is not the most effective way to teach three- and four-year-olds. Although we might gather children to the meeting area for songs, activities, and lots of read-alouds, making our youngest children sit daily for a ten- or fifteen-minute reading lesson followed by independent reading may not be the best use of time.

Although daily whole-class independent reading time may work in kindergarten and first-grade classrooms, it's very difficult for a classroom full of three-, four-, or young five-year-olds to read for the same length of time at the same time. Some students might look at a book for two minutes and then wander away, whereas others might be up for sitting and reading several books over fifteen minutes, yet still other children might have no interest whatsoever in reading a book on a given day. In the world of preschool, this is perfectly fine, perfectly expected, and, well, perfectly preschool.

So instead of a daily and formalized workshop structure, we envision the following components in preschool classrooms:

1. daily picture book read-alouds, including familiar and unfamiliar texts, informational texts, and other genres (we recommend a few a day)

2. occasional whole-group instruction that shows children how they might read familiar, unfamiliar, and informational texts (perhaps once or twice a week) followed by the option to go off and read texts on their own during reading centers or choice time

3. daily opportunities for students to read books independently

4. regular instances where teachers sit down and listen to children read books and teach into what the children are doing

5. occasional times when students share their reading with the class

DAILY READ-ALOUDS

Most preschool teachers read aloud to their children every day. Read-aloud times are often the time teachers and students enjoy most. There are many teacher intentions at work behind the scenes during read-alouds. Sometimes teachers choose to share a favorite story with the children, one that she knows children tend to love. Sometimes, the teacher might choose a book that's related to a theme or project the class is working on at that time. Other times, a teacher might read a book to support a social/emotional goal the children are working on or to address a community need in his classroom. Other read-alouds might be devoted to a book that the teacher is reading each day that week, and then the teacher will move onto a different book for repeated reading the next week. We also hope that there is a read-aloud time tailored to support and inspire children to write their own books. In most preschool classrooms, teachers plan for several read-alouds each day that serve a variety of purposes.

Providing opportunities for children to listen to adults read aloud supports their understanding of what it means to read. If, however, we know we are going to ask students to also read to us, there are ways we can use our regular read-aloud time to lay a foundation and to set an example for our children as they assume the identity of readers themselves. In particular, there are three aspects of read-aloud time that we want to examine: the importance of repeated read-alouds, the necessity of reading aloud informational books, and ways to provide explicit instruction for preschool children during read-alouds.

Repeated Read-Alouds

Children love to hear beloved books read aloud over and over and over. Many parents can name a book that their child wanted to hear at bedtime, night after night, to the point where they were tempted to "lose" the book so they wouldn't have to read it one more night in a row.

When we read aloud a book more than once, we're offering language support for children who may benefit. For example, children who are English language learners are more likely to understand a text and acquire more text language when they have the chance to hear it over and over. Some children have auditory processing challenges, and when they can hear a book more than once, we're providing them with more support for understanding the text. Also, the more chances children get to listen to and look at a particular book, the more they notice, which gives them more to think and talk about. In many ways, every child is supported in some way by deep, ongoing, and repeated experiences with a text.

As readers who are not yet reading conventionally, young children can more quickly and easily access books that they've heard several times. The repeated exposure provides both a reading model and a language model for how the text goes, and children can replicate it in their own reading.

There are a few ways teachers may approach repeated reading of texts. In the Emergent Storybook Reading approach, as developed by Elizabeth Sulzby (and discussed in Chapter 2), teachers select a text that they will read repeatedly at least four or five times within a short period of time—the span of week or two. After the teacher has read the text repeatedly, copies of the book are made available to children to read themselves, and they are invited and encouraged to do so (Sulzby 1985).

Teachers approach repeated readings of texts in other ways, as well. Sometimes a teacher will select a book to read aloud every day for a week or so, chosen because it relates to a theme or project or study. In the fall, for example, in preparation for an autumn harvest project, a preschool teacher might schedule a trip to a pumpkin patch or apple orchard. In accordance with the study and the trip, this teacher might find an engaging text—a book or poem or song—about apples or pumpkins and read that text aloud several times over the course of a week.

Another approach teachers take is to do activity-based read-alouds. One teacher we've worked with had a class full of students who were some of the original *Pete, the Cat* groupies. This fan club began because the teacher had read aloud *Pete, the Cat* on Monday, and the students loved it so much (as the teacher imagined they would) that she decided to read it again on Tuesday. On Tuesday, she encouraged the children to join in on the repeated refrains. On Wednesday, the teacher read it yet again, this time using a cutout of Pete the Cat so students could attach the right color shoes on to Pete as they read each page. On Thursday, she and the children acted out the story as they read it, and on Friday, they read it a final time, this time finding the letter *P* at the beginning of Pete's name on each page.

We encourage teachers to reread books in all of these ways. After spending a week getting to know a book well, children are likely to choose to read it when they have reading time because it's proven to be an engaging book, with predictable text that they know well. They feel confident and comfortable.

To nudge children to the point of confidence and comfort with books, it's so important to make the books we read aloud available for children to read independently. Many teachers create dedicated book baskets that hold these read-aloud books.

In addition to the planned several-days-in-a row repeated readings, there are other more informal ways that teachers can reread books that children love:

- If there's a class leader for each day (or if a child is the birthday kid), one of the perks of that role may be to pick out a favorite book for the teacher to read.
- During choice time, teachers may invite students to join them in the class library to listen to an old favorite book that they haven't heard in a while.
- There might be a Books We Love basket near the front of the room that the teacher uses to find a book to read aloud at rest time, snack time, or at the end of the day.
- When guests visit the classroom, they can pick a book from the Books We Love basket to read aloud to the children.

Whatever approach teachers use at any given time, they'll want to identify which texts students love the best and find time to continue to reread them in short-term bursts and then at times throughout the school year while also making these texts available for children to explore independently.

Reading Aloud Informational Books

The vast majority of books that are read aloud to young children fall into two categories: books that tell a story, like *Knuffle Bunny*, and books that are organized more as a list or accumulation, such as *Brown Bear, Brown Bear, What Do You See?*, or *Dogs* by Emily Gravett.

Both of these kinds of books are wonderful, important, and fun to read to young children. They're often the books children want to hear over and over at home and at school. They aren't the only type of books that they love, however. As we explored in Chapter 6, there are many children who love informational books either to immerse themselves in a topic they're passionate about or to learn about something new.

We've observed Bryan, a four year old, who spent an entire choice time lying belly down on the floor with a Star Wars Lego book opened in front of him as he carefully examines each picture. We watched Valicia carry informational books about flowers back and forth to school for stretches of weeks, to the extent that the pages were worn and sticky and the cover was about to fall off.

As we discussed in Chapter 6, despite their natural inclination to read informational texts, most young children may hear very few informational books read aloud to them. When Matt leads workshops on the teaching of writing for early childhood educators, he'll often ask them to bring or list ten of their favorite picture books they love to read aloud to children. In a session with forty teachers, easily at least a hundred titles would be named, given the fact that some titles get listed by several teachers. Usually, there are no more than ten informational book titles included on the list. In fairness, this doesn't mean that teachers don't have informational books in the classroom, nor does it mean that teachers don't love them. But it could suggest that teachers might not have the natural inclination to read informational texts aloud when they're not tethered to the work of a content area inquiry or unit of study on informational texts.

We encourage teachers to consider increasing the number of informational books they read aloud to children in preschool to capitalize on the reading interest of children who love these types of books. After all, there are some children (and adults) who aren't as captivated by stories, so if we only read stories to children we risk missing an opportunity to increase some children's identities as people who love books.

Another reason it's important to read aloud informational books is simply that we want children to read them aloud to us. When they do so, we'll listen carefully to how they read and offer support for their language development and independence. When we've observed children reading informational books before they can read conventionally, they don't tend to read informational books in ways that sound like informational books at first. They read these books like the stories they are used to hearing. For example, if the first page of an informational text has a photograph of a frog catching a fly on a page about frogs bodies, the child might read, "Once upon a time, the frog stuck out his tongue to catch a fly" or they might say, "The frog caught a fly!"

Children who hear stories frequently know and use story language when they read any text. Children who also get to hear informational texts read aloud to them have a stronger sense for how these books tend to go and how they might sound. But to develop this sense of informational texts, preschoolers need to hear these kinds of books on a regular basis.

To be clear: our strong feelings about exposing prekindergartners to informational books come from what we see occurring authentically in young children's book selections and book interactions. We aren't emphasizing informational books in prekindergarten for the purpose of getting them ready to meet Common Core State Standards that they'll soon encounter. Our rationale for integrating more informational text into preschool classrooms is child-centered and based on our desire to fuel their interests, to increase their engagement with texts, and to expand their vision for what's available.

READ-ALOUD WITH INSTRUCTION:
WHOLE-GROUP LEARNING OPPORTUNITIES

In addition to reasons we've already shared, another purpose for reading aloud to children is to explicitly support them so they can read text themselves. Here are three possibilities for how this type of lesson might sound.

- Imagine that we are reading aloud a familiar book. We begin by inviting children to read along with us. "We all know this book, so please join in and read it with me, if you'd like," we might say. If the book has a repeated refrain or any dialogue passages, the children are likely to jump in and add their voices to those parts. At the end of the book, we might say, "Wow, that was amazing how you all read with me today. You could do that same thing later during choice time and read this book on your own." This is an example of very subtle teaching. We're not teaching a strategy or a skill, per se, but we are teaching them about a possibility—that they can initiate a reading act and read a familiar book by themselves. Although this may be soft teaching, it can be powerful if we consider the cumulative effect of doing this regularly and repeatedly across a year.

- Imagine that we want to read aloud a book that our students don't know. We can just read it aloud, as usual, or we might say to them. "This is the first time we're reading this book. How about if we read it together?" We could turn to the first page, study the picture, and read that (rather than the text) to model how they might approach this task of reading an unfamiliar book. We could turn the page and invite a child to do the same thing, "Would someone study the picture and read this page to us?" Once we read the whole thing together we could say, "Look at how you all figured out what to say for each page by looking carefully at the pictures. That's something you could do during choice time."

- We could also approach this read-aloud with more explicit instruction by saying something like, "Today, I'm going to read this book, but rather than reading the words, I'm going to show you how you can read a book even when you don't know all of the words." We would model for children by looking closely at the pictures and reading them aloud.

In each of these scenarios, it looks like a regular ol' read-aloud. However, the teacher is more explicit about connecting what is going on in the read-aloud with what children can do when they're reading on their own. As always, the tone of this type of read-aloud/lesson should be joyful, engaged, and warm, with natural and authentic instruction.

It's important to say that we don't envision a preschool teacher doing this kind of instructional whole-class read-aloud every single day. Instead, you might use just one or two of your read-alouds each week to focus on helping children read books independently. How much time you devote for this depends on how much time you have with your students. For example, when Matt was a principal, the preschool special education program was two and a half hours long, four days a week. The teachers typically had time for about two read-alouds per day, about eight each week. Because there are multiple purposes for read-alouds, we'd suggest in this case that a teacher devote at least one or two per week to support children's independent reading.

We invite you to watch the following video in which Matt is leading whole-group reading instruction in a preschool classroom. This particular class has been learning about farms and they've grown particularly interested in horses. Their teacher has been reading aloud informational books, and up until this point she has been exclusively focusing her read-alouds on supporting children to learn more about horses and farms. Matt's goal in this lesson is to help them think about ways they can read informational books rather than to help them learn more content knowledge. In other words, Matt's teaching focus isn't farms or horses; it's how to read this type of book.

As you watched the clip, you may have noticed the following:

- Matt begins by prompting children to activate their schema about horses. He reminds them that they already know information about horses, and he suggests that in this new book, they might learn new things or find things they already know about horses. This serves to orient them to the text and suggests that readers can use what they already know to help them read.

- Matt begins by reading the text itself, which is very brief, but he spends most of the time talking about details in the pictures and inviting children to join him. That's what they'll be reading, the pictures, so Matt has chosen to spend more time on the pictures.

- Matt provides vocabulary support around some topic-specific words, such as *stallion* and *mare*. He pauses to ask if they know what the word *gallop* means, and the children generate much language and thinking around that word.

- After a couple of pages in which Matt does the heavy lifting, he makes the move toward giving the children a chance to try the next page, by saying, "If you were reading this book and you saw this page, what would you say?" This is a different question than asking, "What does this page say?" If Matt had phrased it like that, it might have suggested that there's one and only one right way to read that page, and it would have prioritized accuracy rather than meaning making. Matt's word choice is the language of possibility, and it's more inviting than asking young children for a more definitive response.

- At first children aren't sure what to say when Matt issues the invitation, "What would you say?" Matt nudges them by leading them to attend to the picture; he begins by subtly saying, "Look at that horse." He doesn't get much response from that, so he asks a more specific question, "What's this horse doing here?" which offers a bit more support. He takes the children's quick responses "eating" and "eating hay" and pearls them into a possibility for what an informational text might sound like, "Horses eat hay."

- Matt says, "So if you were reading this book, you could say . . ." The word choice is significant here, as well. Matt says, "You *could* say," which also implies that there are possibilities for how they might read it. It implies that you couldn't say "Horses run fast," or "Horses have long tails" for that page because those reads don't match the picture. Of course our goal for all children is that they will read conventionally when they are ready, but for now figuring out what this could say is perfectly appropriate.

After modeling with one book, Matt moves to a book the children haven't seen before and asks them to figure out what each page might say. They've had this experience before with story books, so the new application is trying this with an informational book.

In this part of the clip you may have noticed:

- Matt starts to model elaboration by adding details from the pictures such as, "The baby horse is eating" rather than just "The horse is eating."
- Matt continues to model how he notices details in the pictures. "Look, I notice that the man is holding a rope."
- Children then start to expand their language by saying, "The horse is running with its hair up" rather than just "The horse is running." Matt makes sure to highlight these moments.
- Matt continues to support students in noticing and including details by prompting them to activate their schema—the saddle, horses like apples, showing its teeth, and so on.

Let's imagine the possibilities. Matt may end the lesson by saying, "So when you read an information book like we just did, you can look really closely at the pictures and read what you see." We're not under any illusions that one session of this sort of instruction will set the whole class up to do this work forever more, but we do believe in the cumulative effect of this type of teaching. If we model this attention to pictures and illustrations in our read-alouds and if we take some opportunities to offer explicit instruction during some of our read-alouds, and then if we reinforce this instruction during conferences, we support young children to do more in texts than turn the pages.

Again, we know that any one day of whole-group teaching in preschool may not significantly change how three- and four-year-olds read books. But think about what could happen if a teacher reads aloud one book like this for ten weeks in a row. At the end of those ten weeks students would read books differently. We've seen that happen over and over again.

INDEPENDENT PRACTICE—DAILY OPPORTUNITIES TO READ BOOKS

Children will need plentiful opportunities to interact with familiar, unfamiliar, and informational books on their own to become stronger at reading texts before they can read conventionally. Therefore, it's helpful if the classroom routine includes daily opportunities for children to read and explore books:

- Choice time—Most preschool classes have (or, we think, should have) a time during when children can choose from a variety of activities in the classroom. The library area usually hosts free reading time, one of the choices children can select.
- Center time—In addition to a choice time, some preschool classes have a center time where students rotate through different centers throughout the week.

Teachers offer the Library Center as one of the options children go to regularly to read books and the Bookmaking Center in which children write books.

- When classrooms already have a classroom library, students have many informal opportunities to read, like snack time or at the end of the day when they're waiting for parents or buses. Also, it's helpful to make it clear that anytime students aren't actively engaged in another learning experience, they could go to the library area to read a book.

For some children, the choice to read is easy. Even at this young age, they would spend most of the day in the library center if they could. However, most young children's attraction to reading ebbs and flows. For this reason, it's important that teachers "sell" the choice of reading—which is easier when the classroom is stocked with texts that engage children and when children have opportunities to engage with texts.

At this point, we want to pause briefly to assure readers, whether you're a teacher or a parent, that we do advocate for other kinds of literacy instruction, both implicit and explicit, throughout the day in prekindergarten classrooms. Although our intention in this book is to highlight ways we can support preconventional readers while they are reading texts, we also believe in providing rich, authentic, intentional writing opportunities in preschool so that children have experiences with conveying meaning through composition, developing a strong understanding of letter–sound relationships, encoding words, and learning useful sight words. We encourage teachers to lead shared reading sessions in which they explicitly teach early reading behaviors and provide support to early decoders by attending to the print as appropriate. In classrooms where some children decode with a level of proficiency, we encourage teachers to provide books that allow them to practice and grow as conventional readers . . . because they are ready.

LISTENING AND RESPONDING TO YOUNG CHILDREN AS THEY READ: READING CONFERENCES

The best early childhood educators we know are also the best kid-watchers we know. They observe and listen to children with their hearts and minds. Their responses are tailored to children's personalities, dispositions, quirks, intentions, and development. They meet children where children are and nudge them to new places. Coincidentally but not surprisingly, the work of supporting preschool readers begins with kid-watching—observing as they read texts to figure out ways to support them. Part of this hinges on whether teachers watch children read familiar, unfamiliar, or informational texts. Everything we're thinking about in terms of supporting young readers is dependent on close-up observation. We can't notice what language children use or how independent they are, nor can we help them move forward unless we are sitting beside them, watching and listening as they read.

The good news is that this is fairly easy to make happen in a typical preschool class. We've already established opportunities for children to read books during the day and throughout the week. In classrooms where students have access to books, teachers just need to take advantage of these conditions by sitting down next to a child and asking her to read a book. Whether it's during choice time, in the few minutes after snack, or at the reading center, a teacher does have opportunities to observe a child and to listen in on his reading to nudge him forward.

When we do this, there are several questions that naturally arise.

Who chooses what to read, the teacher or the child?

There are advantages when either the children or the teacher chooses what to read. When children choose the text, they are more motivated to read, and they'll likely bring more energy and enthusiasm to the task. Paying attention to which books they choose reveals children's tastes and interests. We learn whether they prefer stories or informational books. We learn who their favorite authors are, what kinds of books they like, and so on.

There will also be times where we will want to ask children to read a particular book for us to learn more about the child as a reader. For example, if a child only ever wants to read *No, David*, we might want to suggest another title, just to see what this child does in an unfamiliar book or an informational book. Another child might be obsessed with texts with either overwhelming highly detailed illustrations (such as a Richard Scarry book) or sparse illustrations that are hard to wrap language around. In either case, we want the child to read what she wants to read and to have a sense of agency about her book choices, yet, sometimes, we may choose to expand her repertoire.

In short, our default starting point would generally be for children to choose the book, with the teacher asking a child to read a specific book on occasion.

What types of books should we observe them reading?
Familiar, Unfamiliar, Informational?

Over the course of the year we want children to experience reading different types of books, although we don't have a suggested formula or percentage breakdown for how many in each category. Because children will choose many of the books, some will read more of one type than another. We notice what children are reading, and over time we encourage them to read different types of books.

We think this is important because familiar books, unfamiliar books, and informational books all provide children with opportunities to grow as readers. A child who reads only familiar books won't have as many opportunities for rich inferring. He may start to think that he *can't* read a book unless an adult reads it to him first. A child who reads only unfamiliar books won't have as many opportunities to incorporate and use the rich language and specific vocabulary because she has no experience having heard the text read aloud. Another child may worry she can't remember the repeated part of *Caps for Sale* and therefore may believe she can read a book only if she memorizes it.

Exploring a range of books also helps children develop images of themselves as readers who have a point of entry into any kind of text. It's our hope that children feel comfortable and confident enough give any book a chance and for their comfort and confidence to grow as they become more and more proficient.

There is a caveat: no matter what, we want to be aware of children's engagement with reading. If our occasional efforts to encourage young children to read particular types of book over others leads them to frustration or a negative interaction with text, then we may be sacrificing our long-term goal (helping children become a confident readers who loves to read) for a short-term goal (getting children to read different types of books).

Should teachers take notes while children read?

We believe in the power of note-taking, mostly because we've often fallen into the black hole of memory. So much goes on throughout a school day and within a moment, and as much as we think we'll never forget an interaction with a child, soon we're on to the next thing and lo and behold we've forgotten. It's gone. For this reason, we believe it is helpful to take brief notes throughout the day and certainly after listening to children read. We don't want note-taking to detract from the experience and intimacy of interacting with a child, so we usually try to jot our thoughts, observations, and musings after we've left the child. We tend to jot down just a few things that will help us think about what that child can do and isn't doing yet, so we can better support her the next time we meet up with her. With this in mind, here are some things we tend to include in our conference notes:

- Who chose this title? Over time we want to balance child and teacher selection of books. It's hard to maintain a balance unless you know who's been choosing the book.
- What was the child's language and independence level? We need to quickly jot down what we saw the child doing so we can see if there is progress over time.
- What did we teach the child to do? Teachers will usually jot down a simple phrase or fragment, such as "making up dialogue for characters." This is just enough for a teacher to recall what he taught last time and to keep track of what he's taught over time.

There are certainly other things you could write in your conferring notes. You might have a place to note long-term goals for the child or a spot to capture a bit of what they actually said so you could show parents how their child is reading by sharing a specific example. The key is to capture items that will help your next conference build on all you've already done together until that point.

SHARE TIME

This final component is one that we want to handle with care because we don't want to suggest that preschool share times are like share times in kindergarten and first grade but with smaller children. We want to maintain the tone and energy of preschool share times: informal, with certain expectations. We expect that when someone is talking, everyone's attention is on that person, yet the format for a preschool share is much less stylized than the kind of share times older children experience.

At some point during the day many preschool teachers provide a chance for students to share and talk about what they did during the day. This often occurs in the meeting area at the end of the morning or at the end of the afternoon. A student might read a book she wrote at the writing center. Another child might talk about the zoo he was building in the block areas with a group of children, and he might share what they are planning on adding tomorrow. At a time like this it would be natural for a teacher to invite a student to read a book, or a part of a book, that she had read that day in the library center or during reading choice time.

There are two benefits of having children read a portion of a book to the rest of the class. First, it raises the child's identity that she is, in fact, a reader. It's share time, and her teacher just called her a reader, and now she's showing her classmates her reading. It's pretty cool to read on your own or with a teacher. But it's a whole other level to read to your peers, especially with a teacher celebrating the things you did to figure out what to say for each page.

The other benefit is that the child becomes a model for the rest of the class. As much as we say, "You could read a book like this" and then model for them, some children will be much more influenced by seeing their friend read than by a teacher telling them they can do it. Another child's approximation of reading is much closer to what they will do as readers.

To make these reading shares run smoothly, we might guide children by saying, "Alja, would you show your friends what you did when you were reading the book about tigers? Remember the page that you figured out by looking closely at details in the picture?" In most cases, a child would know exactly the part to share, but in case she didn't, the teacher can help to find the part.

There may be a law of diminishing returns if we were to ask a child to read a whole text to the class. In one preschool classroom, the teacher asked a child to share how he read a book during center time that day. Elias stood up and began reading *Piggie and Elephant* to his class by telling the story of the pictures and using some language from the text. The rest of the students watched closely for the first couple of pages, but their attention soon began to dissipate. For this reason, we suggest that when a child reads to classmates, the teacher stays on the lookout for attention drift. If necessary, she might ask the student to read an excerpt or a page or two rather than the whole thing. If most of the other children are attending and engaged, however, it's very empowering for a child to read a whole book to an audience.

It's important for us to say that in addition to the structures and opportunities we've described in this chapter, there are a great deal of other things going on in preschool classrooms that support children's literacy development. From songs to chants to nursery rhymes, from small-motor activities to active recess, from providing time to write and time to inquire, from outdoor play to indoor play, from literacy explorations to literacy adventures—all of these things mean the world to young children who are so ready and able to make meaning in the world around them.

Unfortunately, though, so much tension runs through discussions about education, and that trickles down into the world of preschool. Sometimes contemporary education jargon found in words like *rigor* or *grit* run roughshod over ideas like play-based instruction, even if that's not the intention. The profound influence of the standards movement seems to negate a developmental approach, even if that's not the intention. High-stakes assessments designed by people so far away from the classroom are more valued than the classroom teacher's own observations, even if that is not the intention.

We hope what we've suggested and our intentions are clear and aligned: that you find these ideas about how we might support and nurture prekindergarteners on their reading journey to be both ambitious *and* fair, filled with challenges and comforts, and to be wrapped in both the language of invitation and the spirit of encouragement.

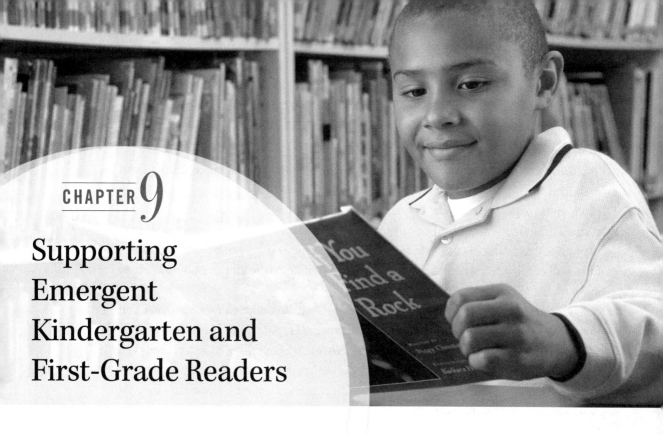

CHAPTER 9

Supporting Emergent Kindergarten and First-Grade Readers

"How does this apply to my first-grade classroom when, from day one, I am focused on helping my kids read with accuracy, fluency, and comprehension so they reach the reading benchmarks we have to check every month?"

"I don't think I have time to let kids read like this when I spend so much time teaching my kindergartners to be able to read the words. They have to be reading at Level C by December in my district."

"I can totally see this in preschool, but in kindergarten? First grade? We've got to get those kids reading the words."

As we outlined this chapter, we didn't plan to deal with these questions until they became hard to ignore—how can we reconcile the pressure kindergarten and first-grade teachers face to get kids reading the words as soon as possible alongside the work of nurturing children's reading identities and teaching them how to make meaning in any text, even those they can't decode?

Our first thought was to simply jump right in and share classroom ideas for supporting children as readers in texts they're not reading conventionally, but it was hard to work around the fact that an educational red alert is issued when children aren't reading

122   I *Am* Reading

at particular levels at various points during kindergarten and first grade. Although we believe it *is* important, necessary, and high-priority work to get children to read conventionally when they are ready, we also believe it *isn't* the only reading instruction to offer.

Continuing to Give Children Time with Texts They Can't Read Conventionally

We imagine that teachers and caregivers can see the benefits of supporting children as readers before they're reading conventionally. It all might sound logical and doable—until children are ready to read conventionally. Once the majority of children in a classroom are ready to read the words, many teachers might feel that this work of continuing to read books without necessarily attending to the print is counterproductive. The questions then become:

> "So, all of my kids are starting to read conventionally and I'm teaching them decoding strategies. Won't it be confusing to also give them books in which they aren't expected to read the words?"
>
> "My children are playing catch-up with letter-sound relationships, basic sight words, and even letter recognition in some cases. Isn't it sort of irresponsible to let them continue to look at books? I feel like I need to scramble to get them reading the words."
>
> "Most of my children have moved toward leveled texts. Shouldn't I spend all of my literacy time supporting their continued growth with leveled texts?"

Again, we want to be clear that we do not suggest withholding or delaying print strategy instruction for children who are ready for it. Making time for children to read anything doesn't replace their time spent with just-right books. Reading just-right books and reading any books are not mutually exclusive. After all, it's important to hold on to the idea that there's much more involved in becoming a well-rounded reader than reading the words with a certain level of accuracy, although that's certainly a big part of it. If we're trying to support children to become well-rounded readers, doesn't it then makes sense for our reading instruction to be well-rounded, also?

If we consider our ultimate goal—that our children become readers who read with accuracy, fluency, and comprehension, but also with joy and intention—then it makes complete sense to give them regular opportunities, with instructional support, to read what they want to read—regardless of whether or not it has a colored dot indicating its level.

Having regular opportunities to make choices is an essential element for student learning (Allington and Gabriel 2012.) It follows that if children have time each day to read books they choose, both just-right book choices and interest-based book choices, and if we can offer instructional support for any kind book they've chosen, they are more likely to become strong, engaged readers than if they are only able to read what we say they can.

Beliefs That Frame Our Reading Work

In Chapter 8 we wrote that the preschool beliefs we described were the same as our beliefs about teaching and learning for kindergarten and first grade. Here are some of those beliefs, modified slightly to more specifically suit kindergarten and first-grade classrooms:

IT'S IMPORTANT TO HAVE A WIDE VARIETY OF BOOKS THAT ARE ACCESSIBLE TO CHILDREN.

The awareness of reading level we described above also permeates the classroom library. There are often colored dot stickers on baskets and on individual books that indicate their text levels. Originally, the intention of the dots was to help children easily find books that they could read with accuracy, fluency, and comprehension. Unfortunately, for some of our youngest readers, those dots can feel less like guides and more like tethers. Stories abound of children saying things like, "My teacher won't let me read those yet," or "I'm an orange dot reader," or "This airplane book doesn't have a dot on it. Can I read it?" or "My mom says I should read the green dot books."

To counter this dot-driven sensibility, we envision classroom libraries also filled with baskets of "dotless" texts that engage students' interests, that expose them to wonderful titles, and that open worlds of possibilities for all children to find themselves within the pages of a book. In many early childhood classrooms there are baskets that contain informational books, innovative and beautiful picture books, books with favorite characters, baskets full of beloved series, and a variety of genres, among many other types of texts. Appendix B provides some ideas for types of books that teachers may want to have on hand in their classrooms.

In addition to a wide assortment of unleveled books, we do also see the necessity of leveled book baskets. It's helpful when a portion of a kindergarten or first-grade classroom library contains leveled books. According to many studies, children need time each day to read books they've selected and can decode with accuracy and read with meaning

(Allington and Gabriel 2012), and a leveled books section of the library makes it easier for children to find these just-right books independently.

Again, it's worth noting that we want children to be strong readers who can decode, comprehend, and read with fluency, but we also want children to have a positive attitude toward reading so that books are something they pursue for pleasure and purpose. We want to empower children to make choices, not just about what book they can choose from a leveled book basket but also what book to choose that goes along with their lives and interests and projects. If a first-grade child chooses eight just-right books per our direction, we also want to support that child in finding books to feed his obsessive interest in ancient Egypt. In other words, we'll encourage and support the child who wants to read the *Eyewitness Book on Ancient Egypt* with as much intention as we'll encourage and support him when he reads his leveled texts.

… we want children to be strong readers who can decode, comprehend, and read with fluency, but we also want children to have a positive attitude toward reading so that books are something they pursue for pleasure and purpose.

Here are some specific considerations about leveled sections in classroom libraries for kindergarten and first grade:

- In kindergarten classrooms, teachers might refrain from putting out leveled books until children are ready to read them. In most kindergarten classrooms in which we've worked, teachers tend to put out the leveled library baskets anytime between October and January, at the time when most of the children in the classroom might be ready to move to conventional reading. If a teacher has children who arrive on day one able to read conventionally, that teacher might assess them to determine independent reading levels and make those leveled books available to them. There's no need to withhold books when children can read them conventionally, nor is there any reason to push leveled books before children are ready to read them. We'll share more ideas about this in the kindergarten section of this chapter.

- In first-grade classrooms, teachers tend to begin the year with an established leveled books section of the library, although children usually don't shop for leveled books for the first couple of weeks of school. We'll share ideas about this later in the first-grade section of this chapter.

- Teachers often ask how many books in a classroom library should be leveled, and we'd say that there is no optimal percentage of leveled books versus unleveled books that we know of, either from research or classroom visits. We've heard 50–50, 75–25, 25–75, and everything else. In general, the more children need support and guidance for choosing books that they can read, the higher quantity of leveled books might be necessary.

WE BELIEVE IN AN EXPANSIVE VISION OF WHAT IT MEANS TO BE A READER, WHICH, IN TURN, CALLS ON US TO EXPAND THE KINDS OF INSTRUCTION OFFERED TO YOUNG READERS.

In the opening to this chapter, we referenced the intensity of the push to get kindergarten and first-grade students to read conventionally and to march through text levels. If our vision of a successful reader is one who can read at a certain level by the end of kindergarten or first grade, then our instructional efforts will be focused on that. If our vision of a successful reader is expanded to be one who not only reads the words with accuracy, fluency, and comprehension but loves to read, shares his thoughts about books, and explores a wide range of texts, then our instruction will need to accommodate the expanded vision. We'll share ideas for this in the kindergarten and first-grade sections that follow.

Reading Workshop in Kindergarten and First-Grade Classrooms

Reading workshop, as envisioned in kindergarten and first-grade classrooms, is one of the points of contrast with preschool classrooms. In preschools, reading time is likely to be an option offered several times a day, and it is likely to occur within a more informal structure. In preschool, children might choose to read during choice time or they may choose reading as a center activity, whereas in kindergarten and first grade, reading workshop is a daily component of their literacy experiences and the whole class participates simultaneously.

Reading workshop is the time in the school day when teachers gather the whole class together to offer instruction to help children read independently. Although children read independently, teachers offer highly tailored and differentiated instruction to individuals and small groups of children. In many kindergarten and first-grade classrooms, all children work within the same unit of study, while receiving whole-class, small-group, and individualized instructional support.

Typically, in both kindergarten and first-grade classrooms, reading workshop follows a blueprint similar to the one shown in Figure 9.1, although the time frames and teaching priorities will certainly be different between kindergarten and first grade, and these priorities change across the year in both grades.

KINDERGARTEN READING WORKSHOP

Let's set a scene: It's the midmorning on the first day of kindergarten in Lynette's room. She's gathering her students into the meeting area for reading workshop. Marisa has just

Whole-class instruction (minilesson) (5–10 minutes)	The teacher gathers the students to a meeting area, often the classroom library space. The teacher presents an assessment-based or unit-of-study-related lesson to the children. The intent is to keep it brief in acknowledgment of young children's limited stamina for attending to whole-class teaching and with respect to maximizing the amount of time children have with books.
Independent reading time (time varies and is aligned with children's stamina)	After the minilesson, the teacher sends the children off to their spots to read independently from a collection of books the students have chosen for themselves, with teacher guidance. While the students read, the teacher confers with individuals and/or meets with small groups of children to offer highly tailored instruction.
Partner reading time (5–15 minutes; time varies and is aligned with children's stamina)	At this time, children meet with a partner to read together and to talk about their books. Again, during this time, the teacher will confer with partnerships or pull together small groups of children for highly tailored instruction.
Workshop share time	The teacher calls the children back to the meeting area to close reading workshop. During share time, the teacher might revisit instruction, highlight children's work, provide an opportunity for children to do new work as readers, and so on.

Figure 9.1

stopped weeping for her momma, and Andre asks her when it will be lunchtime. Again. Ava and Jessa hold hands as they sit practically on top of each other, while E. J. is still finishing his snack. Once they're all gathered, Lynette tells them the good news.

"You know one of the things that's so fun about kindergarten? We get to have time each day for reading workshop! It's time when we get to read books . . ."

"I can't read," Stephen says.

"I can read," Dasha says, pointing her finger straight up in the air next to her face.

"Well, here's the thing. There are lots of ways to read, and we're going to learn about all of them this year. At first, though, we're going to be like explorers. We're going to explore the books we have in our classroom to find some hidden treasures. Books we love. Books that make us laugh. Books that teach us stuff. Books that we want to read a million times. Books that give us ideas. So, today, the first day of school, is also going to be the first day we get to explore our books in reading workshop. Look around at the tables. On each table, there is a bin full of all kinds of books. Today, you'll explore the bins to find books to read, to find treasures. Like this. Watch me."

Lynette walks over to the table nearest to the meeting area and sits in the low chair. She flips through the books in the bin and pretty quickly finds one. "Ooh. This looks good! The cover is cool. This is the one," she says out loud but to herself. She opens it up and begins to look through it, pointing at an illustration while saying something to herself. After a few pages, she stops and returns to the meeting area, holding the book close to her chest.

"Did you see that? I went exploring in that bin, and I found this book that I wanted to read. Did you see? The cover caught my attention. I opened it up, and I was reading the pictures. That's what book explorers do: they find books that catch their attention. Today, you'll all go back to the seat where you had snack. Everyone, take a moment and point to the seat where you ate your snack. You'll go back to that spot and explore the basket on your table to find a book you'll want to look at and read. Ready?" At that point, Lynette got up and began standing near the tables. "OK, if you were sitting at this table near the cubbies, c'mon over. Maya, you, too. If you were at this table near the art area, c'mon over."

Lynette did this for the rest of the tables, until all of the children were at a table and looking through the baskets. Some children very quickly found a book and they sat looking through their text while others were standing up, filing through the bin. At one table, two kids were arguing over whether the bin placement was fair. At the table near the blocks, one child was on the floor exploring blocks, not books. Marisa started weeping for her mama, again.

Lynette walked around the room as the kids explored, encouraging children ("I know you'll find one to read in that basket. There are some awesome books in there."), reassuring children ("Ooh, can I read this picture with you?"), and managing children ("Ezra, we'll explore blocks soon, but now we're exploring books. C'mon, let's find a treasure in here!").

After about five minutes, when Lynette's teacher-sense sounded the alarm that many children's attention might be waning, she says, "Readers, can you, right now, hold up the book that you discovered? Like this." She shows them how. "Everyone, look around at the books your friends discovered. Hey, Kai and Stephen found the same book! They both discovered a *Pete, the Cat* book! How fun!" Lynette quickly gathered the children back into the meeting area.

"So, wow, you guys. You explored books today, and what discoveries you made! Kai and Stephen both found *Pete, the Cat*. What else did you find when you explored the baskets?"

"I found dinosaurs!" Colette said.

"Hey, do you love dinosaurs?" Lynette asked.

Colette nodded.

"And you found a dinosaur book?"

She nodded again.

"I have a T-shirt with them," Eddie added as he pulled his shirt away from his chest to show off the dinosaur on the front.

"Oh, how great that Colette found a book about something she loves. Eddie, if you're into dinosaurs, too, you and Colette might try to find more dinosaur books together. Anyone else find a book about something they love?"

"I found a kitty book," Dasha said.

"You found *Cookie's Week*, didn't you? I saw that one, too. Are you into cats and kittens, Dasha?"

Dasha nodded, and three other children chimed in, "Me, too!"

"Well, how great is that? We found books about stuff we love when we explored the book bins. We found friends who love the same stuff. Guess what? More good news! We're going to explore books again tomorrow to see what else we can find to read."

What a perfectly perfect first day in a kindergarten reading workshop. From start to finish, it was slightly less than sixteen minutes long.

This first day of reading workshop in kindergarten can look like Lynette's, but there are so many other possibilities, too. In any case, children's work during workshop and comfort with reading grows as the days pass. If we were to check in again with Lynette in mid-November, the tabletop book bins would be gone as the books they contained would have been reintegrated into the classroom library baskets. By mid-November, her children would each have their own independent book box containing books they've chosen for themselves. Figure 9.2 describes what a typical kindergarten book box might contain in the mid- to late fall.

As the children work during reading time, teachers confer with them and may pull together small groups. For example, if the teacher knows four children are reading unfamiliar books, she might gather them together for a small-group lesson/reminder about what kind of things readers can do when they read the illustrations.

In Chapter 10, we share ideas for lessons that might be supportive for kindergarten readers during reading workshop.

FIRST-GRADE READING WORKSHOP

To start the year in first grade, many teachers tend to approach reading workshop similar to the way kindergarten teachers do. The workshop in the first two weeks or so follows a similar structure as kindergarten, although children in first grade may be able to stay focused on texts for a little bit longer, especially if they are familiar with reading workshop from kindergarten.

David, a first-grade teacher, uses the whole-class lessons in these first couple of weeks to work with his children on setting a tone and teaching the procedures for reading workshop, on building a community of readers, and on making sure each child is chasing her reading dream. After a whole-class lesson, children head to tables around the room and

Familiar books	Children select these titles from a variety of library baskets. There might be a "Books We've Read Together" basket containing books the teacher has read aloud at least once; a "Star Book" basket, containing books that have been read repeatedly, inspired by the work of Elizabeth Sulzby; a "Shared Reading" basket, containing texts the class has learned through shared reading; or students may find a familiar book that they know from outside of class. Familiar books can be from a wide variety of genres.
Unfamiliar books	Children select these titles from anywhere in the classroom. The criterion is that nobody has read the book aloud to the child before. Unfamiliar books can be from a wide variety of genres.
Informational books	Children select these titles from informational text baskets that might contain books on specific topics (such as "Dinosaur Books") or they might be in a general, all-purpose informational text basket (labeled "Informational Books").
Leveled texts	When children are ready, the teacher will show them where they can find texts in which they will read the words. Children will select several just-right books to read across the week.

Figure 9.2

read books from tabletop book bins that will be out for the first couple of weeks. This time frame allows him to assess children to ascertain independent reading levels and to better understand their interests and dispositions toward reading. In these early weeks, instead of a formalized reading partner time, David devotes a five-minute portion of the workshop for informal buddy reading time, when children turn to the child next to them and chat about their books.

Now imagine that it's early October. The school year is still a young five weeks old according to the calendar, although already in many ways it feels as if summer break was years ago. In the last week or so, David has finished formally assessing his first-grade readers. He has a sense of their reading levels, but just as important, he also has inklings, hunches, and hard evidence about their tastes, quirks, and fears as readers. This information will come in just as handy as quantitative data when David confers and meets with small groups. In addition, David has been observing the social dynamics of his class, especially in the last couple of weeks as the children have grown more familiar with each other and comfortable in the world of their first-grade classroom. David uses this information, in conjunction with what he knows about the children as readers, to plan out how his children will be paired for partner time in reading workshop.

The instruction for the first few weeks of school focused on learning the procedures of workshop, building a reading identity and reading life, building expectations for a healthy reading community, and getting to know ourselves and each other as readers, thinkers, and talkers about texts. But now, the class as a whole is ready for the next unit of study, which is largely focused on word-solving. Of course, David has a vast range of readers who sit before him in the meeting area, including a handful of children who can read the words in chapter books, a few children who are still working to secure some very early reading skills such as one-to-one match, and three English language learners who do not share the same home language.

At the beginning of this unit, a rite of passage is for children to get their own book boxes, which are actually unused pizza boxes donated by the local pizzeria. The children have decorated these book boxes, so there are stickers and photographs, designs and drawings that distinguish one box from another. There are stacks of six to eight of these book boxes in a few places around the room, so when it's reading time, children know exactly where to go get their box before settling into their reading spot.

At this point, each child's reading box is filled mostly with just-right books. David has given the children a little "shopping list"—an index card with a colored dot and a number inside. For example, Emi's shopping list has an orange dot with "6" and a yellow dot with a "2" written inside. This means that Emi will find six just-right books in the orange dot baskets and two in the yellow dot baskets. The children all use a shopping list tailored specifically for of each of them during the first couple of weeks of this unit, while they are getting used to the system of shopping for just-right books each Monday. David anticipates that soon, most children won't need this visual reminder and he plans to phase out the shopping lists, except for children who might still need this support.

In addition to the leveled books, the children also have a couple of books they want to read, regardless of whether or not they can read them conventionally. Gregory, whose current independent reading ranges around a Fountas & Pinnell Level E/F has the brand-new Scaredy Squirrel book along with an Eyewitness book about baseball in his book box. David makes sure children have time each day to read these books, in addition to their daily time to read just-right books.

Figure 9.3 shows how David's first-grade class reading time tends to go, once children are shopping for just-right books.

In David's classroom, "read anything" time happens daily, often right after reading workshop share time. The children either go back to their spots to pick out texts from their book boxes, or they choose to read something from the classroom library. David leaves this rather open—both in terms of what children read and how they read. In his classroom

Whole-Class Instruction

(5–15 minutes)

Independent Reading Time

(10–25 minutes, or as long as children can stay focused)

Children are reading just-right books while the teacher confers and meets with small groups.

Partner Reading Time

(5–15 minutes)

Children meet with their teacher-assigned partner each day to talk about just-right books.

Workshop Share Time

(5–10 minutes)

Teacher gathers children back to meeting area to share, learn, talk, process, reflect, and so on.

Read Anything Time

(5–15 minutes, or as much time as possible)

Children can read anything from their book box, including the books they can't read conventionally. The teacher confers with children about their books. This may occur right after reading workshop or at another time of the day, every day.

Figure 9.3

on this day, Sasha uses her free reading time to continue reading the Magic Tree House book she started during reading workshop, while James and Roland lie side by side looking through an informational text about outer space, focusing specifically on a section about the planets.

In much the same way as he circulates around the room for independent reading time when children are reading just-right books, David also works with as many children as he can during the read anything time, conferring with them about their texts ("Of all the Magic Tree House books you've read so far, how does this one rank? One of the best? So-so?"), encouraging them ("Hey, you know, you can study this diagram and get information about the planets. Like look at this one—it's teaching us something about the planets' sizes"), nudging them toward more sophisticated language levels, ("Ella, would you read this page aloud to me, including all of the details? That will help me know what's going on."), and trying to figure them out ("Daniel, I noticed that you're walking around a lot today. What's up?").

Whole-Class Instruction

Almost every day in reading workshop, teachers begin by leading a whole-class minilesson. This five- to fifteen-minute lesson provides children with instruction to support their independent reading. Given the fact that much of a teacher's instructional energies are devoted to teaching kindergarten and first-grade children to read conventionally, it might be hard to imagine finding time to teach minilessons that support children in reading texts that they may not be able to read conventionally.

This is compounded by the simple fact that once children begin to learn how to read the words, they may *want* to only read the words. Some children might feel wary of books that look "too hard," especially when they're encouraged to seek out and read only just-right books. They wield their newly acquired conventional reading power and enjoy the accomplishment of figuring out the words on the pages. We support that.

On the other hand, there are so many high-quality picture books and informational texts that young children might not be able to accurately decode but that still provide opportunities for engagement and strategy use, books that pique a child's interest or set off a newly discovered passion. Even as he was learning to read conventionally and reading up the levels, first-grader Rowan spent many hours of his early reading life lost in books about superheroes and Greek and Norse mythology, looking at comic books until they were falling apart, and studying the pictures in graphic novels. He loved Calvin and Hobbes before he could read it. For the most part, he couldn't read the words in these books very easily, but he sure did spend lots of time reading the pictures, making sense of the illustrations and the story lines. His passions were realized in these texts, and he learned so much about the pleasures of reading because he had these texts in his life. We support that, too.

We suggest that teachers strive to strike some sort of balance in the ratio of time spent between just-right reading, when children read books they can read with at least 98 percent accuracy, fluency, and comprehension, and free-range reading when children read what their hearts, minds, and moods desire—which may or may not include just-right books. Of course, out of necessity, this balance may skew in favor of more time spent with just-right books, as well it should when we're teaching children to read conventionally. Yet, even when children are learning to read words and make meaning in leveled text, we believe in the power of complementing just-right reading with daily opportunities for children to read whatever they want.

When children are free-range reading, it's important that teachers treat these time frames as teachable moments, doing the things they would do during just-right reading time: conferring with individuals or pulling small groups of children to support their work or to teach them something new. Figure 9.4 shows some ways we can harness the power

Some Possible Teaching Points for Free-Range Reading Time

Print and Vocabulary Support

Unfamiliar Book
- Sometimes we might read texts that are way too hard, but we can often find some words we might know and we can use those words to help us figure out how the book goes.
- If you're just not sure what a part of the book is about, see if there are some words that could help you figure it out.
- When you're reading a text without really reading the words, think like the writer did and use specific language. Instead of saying, "She walked in the park," you could say, "The little girl skipped past the flowers and across the bridge."

Familiar Book
- If you know the book because it's been read aloud to you before, use a mix of what you remember about the story as well as words you know to help you read through it.
- If there are repeating parts you know by heart, try to find the words in the text and read them as you say the part.
- You can use your memory for how the book goes and find the words on the pages that go along with what you remember.

Comprehension Support

Unfamiliar and Familiar Books
- We can try to figure out what characters might be thinking or feeling by looking for clues in their facial expressions and body language (inferring).
- We try to figure out the flow of the story by looking at how one page connects to the next (monitoring for meaning).
- We can use our schema and connections to understand what's going on (activating prior knowledge and making connections).
- We can figure out what's important on each page and use that to help us figure out what's going on in the text (determining importance).
- We can grow ideas about the text by thinking to ourselves, "What is this about?" (summarizing).
- We can reread books by reexamining the pictures to find things we didn't notice the first time.
- We can track a character throughout a book to try to get to know that character really well.

Fluency Support

Unfamiliar
- We can talk like the character might talk by looking at her expression and what's going on.
- What can consider the tone/mood the illustrations convey and think about how we can use our voices to match the tone/mood as we read it.
- We can change our voices to match the action in the story.
- If we see lots of bold words or words in all capital letters, it might mean we should read those parts in big voices.
- We can read things so that they sound like a story by using story language that we know.

Familiar
- We can use what we know about how the book goes to guide our voices to read it with expression.

Informational Text Support

Unfamiliar and Familiar
- We can study the pictures in informational texts and say, "I notice . . . and I'm thinking . . ."
- We can think about what we already know about a topic to help us learn more as we study the pictures.
- We can look at the pictures on a page and try to figure out what the author wants us to know.
- We choose informational texts for lots of reasons, including a desire to become an expert and the desire to learn something new.
- There are lots of ways to read informational texts.
- We can look for words we might know as we look through informational texts.
- We can find things that we want to talk about with someone else.

Figure 9.4

Some Possible Teaching Points for Free-Range Reading Time (Continued)

Habits and Behaviors to Support	Response to Reading Support
• There are lots of things people consider when they choose which books to read. • When we reread a text we know, we can pay close attention to when we notice new things or have new thoughts about it. • We can recommend books to other people if we think they'd be interested in them. • We can pay very close attention to what we're thinking as we read.	• We can share our reading with others by inviting them to join us as we explore a book. • We can finish a book and think about what we would want to say about it. • As we read, we can use sticky notes to mark places that we want to think about more or talk about. • Books can inspire us in some way—to try something, to learn something, and so forth.

Figure 9.4 (Continued)

of free-range reading time to teach children strategies and habits that will also be helpful when they read just-right books. These teaching points can be used during whole-group teaching, small-group instruction, individual conferences, or share time.

We'd like to share a video of Soroya leading a whole-class lesson in a kindergarten reading workshop during one of the first few weeks of school.

Clip 9.1 *Kindergarten Whole Group*

http://smarturl.it/Clip9.1

In this lesson, Soroya is teaching children to use action sounds to read their books. She makes the wise choice of modeling with *Mrs. Wishy-Washy*, a book the children know very well, which suggests that already, so early in the school year, Soroya has read it several times during shared reading. Because the children know the book, it's easier to focus on the teaching point—they aren't distracted by the novelty of a brand-new story.

Soroya moves through the architecture of a minilesson as described by Lucy Calkins and colleagues in many books within their units of study series. She makes a clear teaching point—readers can use action sounds to read a story. As she makes the teaching point, Soroya also embeds reminders of the other things they've learned to do as they read by themselves—touch and tell about the characters, make the characters talk, and tell what's going on in the story.

Soroya goes on to model how to do this work. She thinks aloud, "I think when her hands go in the air, it goes like this—whoosh." She tries a couple of more action sounds while skillfully contextualizing them in the story ("He's got water everywhere, I think that's what it sounds like"), before she turns it over to the children for them to try.

Soroya issues an invitation to the children to join her to make an action sound and then she invites them to help her figure out what a part might sound like before giving the kids a chance to try it on their own. She sets up this opportunity for children's engagement by providing the context for the noise in that part (4:20) by asking them to think of the sounds they might hear on this page before just prompting them to make the sound.

What else do you notice as you view this?

We've also included a video of Krissy, a first-grade teacher who is leading a whole-class lesson later in the year about how first graders can read an informational text even if they can't read all of the words. As you watch, you'll notice the clarity of Krissy's teaching point, and the way she moves smoothly through a research-based minilesson structure that begins with a connection and statement of the teaching point and continues with a teaching demonstration before providing children with time to try what she has taught. At the end, Krissy links what her class learned in that lesson to the work they can do as readers.

Clip 9.2 *First Grade Whole Group*

http://smarturl.it/Clip9.2

If teachers agree that this sort of daily free-range reading time with instructional support is valuable for young readers, the challenge is to find ten to fifteen minutes a day for it to take place. Here are some possibilities:

- **Morning arrival:** At schools where children arrive at the classroom in bunches, teachers have found that free reading time is a soft way to welcome everyone as they arrive. Once children arrive, they can make their way to books. In other neighborhood schools, children arrive by a variety of transportation methods—some walk to school with their caregivers, others ride their bikes or take a school bus. They don't always arrive all at once. If this is the case, after children unpack they read something by themselves or with a friend while they await the morning meeting or first activity. Many teachers say that free-range reading offers a gentle, calming start to the school day when children's first work is to "Find a book, find a spot, and lose yourself in your reading."

- **After reading workshop:** Some teachers prefer to attach free-range reading time to the end of reading workshop. Children are already in the reading frame of mind, and it may feel seamless to give them an extra ten to fifteen minutes to read whatever they want. To carve out this time, teachers might keep their minilessons a bit shorter once or twice a week, they might shorten the share time a couple of days a week, or they might choose to substitute read anything time for partner reading time once a week. We recommend trading partner time for free-reading time no more than once a week because children need time daily to talk with others about their books (Allington and Gabriel 2012).

- **Other found times:** On certain days of the week, teachers might have ten- to fifteen-minute pockets due to the variation in their schedules. Some teachers offer free-reading time right after lunch or recess as a way of giving everyone the time they may need to recalibrate their energies for the classroom. Other teachers that have staggered dismissals save the last fifteen minutes of the day as read anything time. If recess is canceled due to weather or other reasons, teachers may choose to offer free reading time as a reasonable alternative.

Although we advocate for fitting in a free-range reading time whenever possible, we recognize that it can be difficult to always confer with readers during this time. For example, if a teacher welcomes children in the morning with a version of free-range reading, it may be hard to both circulate among arriving children and confer with reading children amid the typical morning chaos of collecting permission slips, checking homework, drying tears, listening to children's stories, and so on. If a teacher finds it hard to sit and talk with children during free-range reading time, we would suggest looking at the daily schedule for other options. The conferring part of this time is worth it, for both the teacher and the child.

Other Times in the Day When We Can Support Readers

In addition to reading workshop, kindergartners and first-graders have other experiences with texts and opportunities for literacy growth. The following lists include what many literacy experts consider to be the components of a balanced literacy framework, and we've also included what we consider to be literacy-enhancing parts of the day.

Balanced Literacy Components
- reading workshop
- writing workshop
- shared reading/shared writing
- interactive read-aloud/emergent storybook read-aloud/storytime
- word study
- interactive writing

Literacy-Enhancing Components and Content Areas
- choice time
- social studies inquiry
- science inquiry
- arts (including visual, dance, music, performing)
- center time

The literacy components provide opportunities to teach specific skills and strategies that readers need to become accurate decoders, deep comprehenders, and fluent readers. By design, they are meant to give young readers lots of literacy experiences, strategic instruction, and exposure to a wide variety of texts.

The literacy-enhancing components, on the other hand, work to support children as readers and writers for specific purposes, often to learn content and understand the world around them. For example, when a kindergarten classroom is studying families for a social studies inquiry or a first-grade classroom is studying insects during a science inquiry, teachers read aloud texts and model how readers can learn about topics through reading. These texts then become mentor texts for when children will write informational books.

Although it's not in the scope of this book to write in great detail about all of the balanced literacy components or the literacy-enhancing components, we do want to clarify three things on the chart: interactive read-aloud, emergent storybook read-aloud, and storytime.

INTERACTIVE READ-ALOUD

This is the time in the day when the teacher reads aloud to children to model the work, play, and behaviors that characterize an active, engaged reader. According to Allington and Gabriel (2012), this is an essential part of every school day.

During interactive read-aloud time (which is also known as read-aloud with accountable talk), the teacher reads aloud a text. While reading, she models the kinds of things strong and engaged readers might do. She thinks aloud about the text in front of the children ("Oh, Trixie is so upset. I can just tell by looking at her face and by how she's pleading with her daddy."). She provides opportunities for the children to talk about the text by prompting what many teachers call "turn and talk" time. For example, a teacher might say, "Trixie is so upset, and her daddy is trying to figure out what she's saying. Look closely at her daddy. What might he be thinking right now? In a moment, turn and tell your partner." After finishing the text, the teacher usually facilitates a whole-class conversation about it. This book talk typically includes the use of a variety of reading strategies, such as retelling, summarizing, inferring, close reading, connecting, interpreting, and so on. Book talks during read-aloud also include a variety of strategies for having a strong conversation, including instruction about being an active listener and a clear talker.

Teachers tend to select a wide variety of texts for interactive read-aloud time, from picture books to chapter books, from informational texts to fantastic stories, from biographies to realistic fiction, from concept books to poetry. The implicit (and sometimes explicit) instruction during read-aloud includes the following:

- strategies to pick books
- comprehension strategies and fix-it strategies
- vocabulary and concept knowledge acquisition
- habits and behaviors of engaged readers
- response to reading (i.e., sketching, talking, dramatizing)
- and so much more

EMERGENT STORYBOOK READING

This is an approach developed by Elizabeth Sulzby, which we briefly described in Chapter 2. In short, teachers select an engaging picture book that meets a variety of criteria. These books are typically narrative picture books with strong relationships between the text and the illustrations, repeated refrains, and dialogue, perhaps, and text that is interesting to children. Teachers read aloud these storybooks repeatedly over four or five days. Each time the teacher reads an emergent storybook, which many teachers call "star books," the children grow more familiar with the story and more knowledgeable about how it goes. The more the teacher reads these books aloud, the more children may join in on the dialogue passages or the repeated refrains. Once they've heard the story at least four or five times, the teacher makes multiple copies available to the children to read on their own while she confers to support and instruct them (Sulzby 1985).

These books and this approach are supportive for all children, including those who are English language learners or those who have auditory processing challenges. Because the texts are read aloud over and over within a short span of days, children who may typically struggle to understand or to hold on to the story have an easier time with these texts.

STORYTIME

We first heard our friend, Cheryl Tyler, make a distinction between interactive read-aloud and storytime. Cheryl said that storytime is a time of day when the teacher and the children are immersed in the world of a book, in much the same way as when a caregiver is reading to a child. The teacher hasn't chosen the book to make a preplanned teaching point or to meet a curricular agenda. Instead, the teacher and his students are enjoying a text together, and the teacher is following the students' interests and enthusiasm for the story.

Storytime often takes place during a "found time" in the day. It's thundering and lightning, and the class won't be going out for recess? That's a great time for storytime. Children finish cleaning up quickly after their inquiry centers? That's a great time for storytime. It's a child's birthday, and there's a new "no cupcake and no junk food" rule in your school? That's a great time for storytime. Actually, we believe it's always a great time for storytime, although we do realize that there are other things that need to happen in a school day.

When the instructional emphasis is largely focused on getting children to read conventionally as early as possible, children's literacy experiences in kindergarten and first grade become dominated by a sense of level. Years ago, information about a child's reading level stayed mostly in the pages of a teacher's plan book or conferring notes. These days, however, children's reading levels are much more public. In many places they are posted on data walls for anybody to see. There are some school and district administrations that expect teachers to plot children's reading levels on these public graphs in their efforts to encourage children (and teachers) to "keep on trying!" In some places, teachers are rewarded or punished depending on whether their students' reading levels meet benchmarks across the year. These days, in addition to her teacher, a child's family, classmates, school principal, district-level coordinators, and any classroom visitors may have access to her reading level and data at any moment in time.

Even without this pressure, it's hard not to think of reading levels when we think about young readers. There are no two consecutive school years in which children are expected to grow more as readers, level-wise, as they are from the start of kindergarten to the end of first grade, so the push to get children reading conventionally, which means decoding words and moving up text-level ladders, drives literacy instruction in most kindergarten and all first-grade classrooms. For this reason, we understand that some teachers in these grades might wonder whether it's worth their while to spend any time working with children on how to make meaning in books they can't yet read and on supporting them to develop well-rounded reading identities.

When our highest priority is to help kids march up through reading levels, the cycle of reading instruction turns like this: we assess children to find out what level they can read independently, and we direct them to baskets containing just-right books, which intentionally limit their selections. We teach them strategies to support their movement through levels, and for early-level readers, a large portion of the instruction is angled toward word-solving. What ends up missing, then, is the idea that individuals read for many purposes that have nothing to do with level—including reading for pleasure. Also missing is the opportunity to explore the wide variety of texts and genres available. Typically, when we are in the business of fast-tracking children through reading levels, the books they see are almost exclusively leveled text. The act of reading becomes a race to the top, where books are mere stepping-stones, and the identity of a reader is mostly connected to the color of the level dots on his books.

To be fair, we want to acknowledge that the vast majority of early childhood teachers with whom we work are trying with all of their might to maintain a sense of joy and to protect their children's growing identities as readers from the tyranny of levels and data. It's not that these teachers are level-phobic or antidata; they just use levels and data the way they were intended—their data inform their instruction, and text-leveling systems guide their children toward finding books that are just right.

We also want to be clear that we're not suggesting that teachers reduce their efforts to support children as conventional readers when the children are ready, nor do we intend to deemphasize the importance of teaching children strategies to figure out words when they are ready to do so. We aren't advocating for teachers to peel off the dots from their leveled books or that children "free-range" read all day in kindergarten and first grade.

What we hope to convey in this chapter is the idea that there is so much more to a reading identity than the color of the dots on one's books, and that when children are young and just beginning to enter the formal world of reading, we are wise to create classroom conditions where learning to *love* to read is prioritized as much as learning *how* to read.

CHAPTER 10

Yearlong Planning

s we write this chapter, it's late August and another school year is just beginning. Parents are flooding social media with videos and photographs of their
children posing in their first-day-of-school outfits and supersized book bags.
Teachers have set up their rooms with care, anticipating the new community of
children they are about to teach. The children are wide-eyed or teary-eyed, or
both. Some are confident and eager to take on the new world of school; others
are full of worries and wishing they could postpone it just a little bit longer.

No matter how children begin a school year, so much will change for them by the
time they finish it. Whether they're in half-day preschool or full-day kindergarten, their
teachers and caregivers know that young children will grow and change in so many ways
over the year.

Some of this growth is quantifiable, assessable, and easily made public. We can compare
children's fall and spring assessments and hope to see steadily upward lines of growth.
We can look at children's early-in-the-year writing and drawing samples alongside their

end-of-the-year samples and notice more sophisticated compositions and illustrations, more conventionally spelled words, and more legible handwriting.

Although many children in one classroom may share the same reading levels or mastery of sight words or accumulation of conventionally spelled words, their developing identities as learners and their attitudes toward literacy are idiosyncratic, nonlinear, and quite variable. This development, from the first month to the last, is not as quantifiable but is no less important. Children's dispositions toward their school work, their identities as learners, and the ways they deal with challenges are well worth our attention. It's important, then, that teachers plan instruction and create environments that are purposefully considerate of children's personal and emotional growth, in addition to planning instruction and conditions that ensure academic progress.

In Chapters 8 and 9, we shared some beliefs about learning and ideas for supporting young children's literacy development before they're reading conventionally in preschool and kindergarten and when they're reading conventionally in kindergarten and first grade. We suggested some (not all) structures and reading opportunities we can provide, ranging from regular storytimes and read-alouds to centers, choice time, and reading workshop. We offered ideas for teaching reading to a whole group of children as well as for conferring with an individual child in that important moment when we sit beside her as she interacts with a book.

In this chapter, we consider all this reading work through a wide-angle lens. We'll take an August-to-June view—and think about how to support, encourage, and instruct children about reading and learning over time, during that precious time before they're reading conventionally.

Supporting Readers Who May Not Be Reading the Words . . . Yet

As we think about teaching across a school year, it's important to hold fast to our beliefs and priorities as we plan instruction that reflects them. It can be easy to forget what's really important when everything feels *really* important. Most of us begin the year recognizing we're teaching children, not just readers or writers or mathematicians, and we work hard to create safe and inviting learning communities. Soon, though, once our community has learned each other's names and has a shared sense of personalities and expectations, we feel compelled to shift gears and press forward, focused mostly on matters of student achievement and academic growth. Although these matters are certainly important, we don't think they're all that's worth pursuing.

We believe teaching doesn't have to be an either-or proposition, where we have to choose between nurturing instruction or achievement-first instruction.

We believe teaching doesn't have to be an either-or proposition, where we have to choose between nurturing instruction or achievement-first instruction. Our connections with and instruction of young children need to be considerate of their humanity as much as their learning needs.

When we hold on tightly to our beliefs about working with young children while considering the learning opportunities we might provide, our priorities are to help children develop:

- secure and confident identities as readers and writers
- healthy learning dispositions for trying new things and taking risks
- positive attitudes toward books and reading and writing
- meaning-making skills for reading or composing any kind of text
- speaking and listening skills
- social skills through robust play, both inside and outside the classroom, and learning partnerships across the day
- letter and word recognition, knowledge of letter–sound relationships, and word-solving strategies when they are ready

These priorities infuse our instruction throughout the year (Figure 10.1).

Moving Through the Preschool Year with Meaning Making on Our Minds

Imagine a child as he takes his first steps. He steps once, twice, three times before toppling into the loving arms of a caregiver. After a day or two of wobbly stop-and-start walking, imagine if his mom carried him over to the bottom step of a staircase. As she takes a seat up on the fourth step, she encourages him to walk up the stairs to meet her. "C'mon, sweetie, walk up the stairs! You're going to have to do it sometime. C'mon, you can do it. Walk up to mommy!" This scene on a staircase is an exaggeration of an all-too-common sensibility: "You're going to have to do it eventually, so you might as well start now."

We Prioritize the Growth and Development of:	How Might We Facilitate the Development of These Priorities in Our Classrooms?
Secure and confident identities as readers and writers	Regular invitations to read and write during centers, choice time, and workshops; modeling of reading and writing; offering options for what to read and write; acknowledging children's growth
Healthy learning dispositions for trying new things and taking risks	Acknowledging and celebrating when children try new things; valuing mistakes and showing how to use them to grow; regularly introducing new options within familiar structures (i.e., media options during art; new math games; genre options for reading and writing, inquiries, and center time choices)
Positive attitudes toward books and reading and writing	Regular read-alouds of beloved books; time each day for children to read or write whatever they want; providing options to develop children's sense of agency as readers and writers
Meaning-making strategies for reading or composing any kind of text	Creating a culture of understanding throughout the day; modeling how to ask for clarification; teaching comprehension skills; inviting children to acknowledge when something is hard to understand
Speaking and listening skills	Time for informal conversations and self-initiated conversations between children; a variety of talk opportunities (negotiating, explaining, persuading, discussing, and so on.); formalized structures for talk—partnerships during reading and writing; read-aloud conversations; modeling the habits of effective speakers and active listeners
Social skills	Time for play, both inside and outside the classroom; discussions of classroom social and community issues
Letter and word recognition, knowledge of letter–sound relationships, and word-solving strategies when children are ready	Explicit and implicit instruction through shared reading, word study time, letter formation time, minilessons; opportunities to orchestrate strategies and problem-solve during choice time, center time, and reading and writing workshops

Figure 10.1

We know this staircase example sounds silly, but versions of this "rushed readiness" happen all the time in preschool and elementary classrooms—from preschool children who do worksheets throughout the day (because they must learn to sit still and complete their work for kindergarten), to kindergartners who practice bubbling in answers (because they'll take bubble-answer assessments in the next few years), from second-graders who learn to touch-type on keyboards that stretch their little fingers to the limits (because third-grade tests are administered on a computer), to fifth-graders who spend months on test preparation (because success on high-stakes tests will position them for middle school placement, which will lead to better high school options, which can get them into Ivy League schools, and so on).

We can't help but be reminded of the age-old question: just because children can, does it mean they should? What are we giving up when we add touch-typing practice into a jam-packed second-grade schedule? What part of a kindergartner's day is traded out so she can practice filling in bubble answers? So many tasks, challenges, and standards are pushed down into early childhood to "get kids ready" for some nebulous and always rising expectation down the road. But when we're always getting children ready, we're not seeing them as they are.

On the other hand, when we meet young children where they are and move them along with ambitious but fair expectations, they'll be ready for the challenges ahead. The hard part is that not all young children are ready for the same things at the same time. When we stand beside children at their own individual starting points—instead of teaching from the finish line and expecting them to race there—we must observe often and differentiate constantly. In this way, we prioritize teaching children over teaching stuff.

We don't view preschool classrooms as training grounds for kindergarten, a view we acknowledge is at odds with some contemporary initiatives for preschools. The preschool years are brief and precious, and we want to teach in a way that's considerate of who children are and what they can do at that time, rather than focusing solely on who they need to be and what they have to do in the future.

What does this mean for preschool reading work? Throughout the day, children sing songs, participate in storytelling, explore letters and words, and make books. They use and create texts for their inquiries and play. Instead of a formalized reading workshop when every child is reading at the same time, we provide opportunities for children to read several times a day during choice and center time. We also find many opportunities to teach during read-aloud and shared reading. We show children how the things we do as we read to them are things they can do when they read by themselves either in school or at home.

Because children aren't all reading at the same time in a preschool classroom, when we think across a year, we tend not to plan formal "units of study" more typical in kindergarten and first grade, but we do have intentions and particular emphases at different points of the year.

EARLY IN THE PRESCHOOL YEAR

When we start the year, our focus is on helping children establish images of themselves as a capable readers, writers, artists, pretenders, block builders, scientists, snack time cleaner-uppers, and so on. For readers specifically, we teach children that they can, in fact, read books they know and books they don't know, even if they can't yet read the words. We read a variety of books aloud, including familiar books, unfamiliar books, informational texts, and texts that represent different genres, such as concept books, wordless books, activity books (look-alike books, Where's Waldo-type books, etc.). As we read, we make asides to children such as, "Oh, hmm. Let me see what's going on in this picture. That can help me read this page." And while we read texts conventionally in front of children, we also pause and muse on different pages so we model all the things children can do when they're reading by themselves or with a friend, at school or at home.

We also help children develop healthy and highly functional reading habits. We teach them ways readers choose books and ways they might share books with others. We celebrate their individual choices ("Oh, Michael, I think you've read every single insect book we've got!"), habits ("Charlie, can you show Maryam how you use a bookmark to save your place?"), and social dispositions around reading ("Did anyone else hear Nevaeh and Alyse acting out *Piggie and Elephant* today in the reading center?"). We can set up structures so that each child has at least one reading time each day, and we can encourage children to choose reading by talking about all the reasons people might choose to read instead of doing much anything else.

THE REST OF THE YEAR IN PRESCHOOL

After building a community of readers who choose to read and know what they can do with books, our instructional intentions shift toward helping children get stronger as readers and become more independent with books. During these months, we observe what children are already doing as readers and instruct them about what might come next. We consider what most or many children are doing in reading and what they may need to move ahead, then we focus on those needs during read-aloud, shared reading, and weekly minilessons.

Additionally, you might find that different times of year lend themselves to particular types of reading. In many preschool classrooms, for example, children make picture books right from the first days of school, (Ray and Glover 2008; Glover 2009) so teachers might read books aloud that support children's bookmaking, pointing out different illustration possibilities, for instance, or highlighting a story structure to give children schema for writing their own storybooks.

Although we advocate for frequent informational texts read-alouds related to children's interests, these books are especially important when preschool children are engaged in a particular inquiry or project. Teachers read aloud books to explore the topic of study and include these books as choices for reading during center and choice time. At one preschool, for instance, children were studying a pond outside their classroom to make sure it would be a good habitat for their tadpoles to grow into frogs. They read many books about ponds and frogs, including different kinds of informational texts, ABC books, and printed pages from related websites. This reading introduced children to important content, but it also gave them experience with reading skills they can transfer to any text they're reading, whether it's about frogs, trucks, or superheroes. Reading books to children related to their projects and inquiries provides them with important schema, increases their motivation and engagement, and shows them how they can learn about anything through reading. Later in this chapter, we'll highlight some possible teaching points that will provide preschool teachers with a vision for how they might support preschool readers across the year.

Moving Through Kindergarten and First Grade with Meaning Making on Our Minds

Many kindergarten and first-grade teachers make curricular decisions for a year of reading workshop based on preplanned units of study either created by a team of teachers within the school or based on units published in professional texts. Reading units of study typically support kindergarten and first-grade readers in a variety of ways—from units that teach children strategies to read words to units in which they explore a certain genre; from units that sharpen and deepen children's comprehension skills to units focused mostly on fluency (Collins 2004). In a unit of study, the teacher leads a daily whole-class minilesson, after which the children have time to read independently and with a reading partner. While the children read, the teacher may confer with individuals or pull together a small group to teach highly tailored and differentiated skills and strategies.

Although many kindergarten and first-grade reading workshops follow this familiar structure and are organized by units of study, there are differences related to daily schedules, instructional decisions, curricular decisions, and priorities. The contemporary pressure to teach children to read conventionally as quickly as possible can take up so much instructional time and planning energy. Still, we believe children benefit from opportunities to read and explore familiar, unfamiliar, and informational texts they can't yet read conventionally. There are ways teachers in kindergarten and first grade can provide adequate time for children to read leveled texts that match them as readers, while also finding opportunities for children to read texts they've chosen for their own reasons, whether or not they can read them conventionally.

We believe it's important for children to have consistent opportunities and adult support to read any book they choose, regardless of level, because:

- **Texts in the real world aren't leveled.** When a child goes into an independent bookstore or a public library, chances are slim the books there will be organized by level as they are in school. It's vital, then, that we show children strategies to make meaning and engage with any book they choose, whether or not they can read it with accuracy. This doesn't negate the idea nor contradict the proven research that children need to read just-right books as they learn to read. We're suggesting children have time to read both just-right books and books they've chosen for any other reason.

- **Choice motivates.** Peter Johnston (2004) reminds us how important it is that children have a sense of agency in their learning, which includes opportunities to make self-initiated choices. When children are empowered to choose what they read, they are more likely to be engaged with the texts in their hands. If the only books children have access to are the ones we've decided they should read, we reduce their sense of agency, and in many cases, we risk reducing their motivation.

- **Rich picture books and informational texts give children more opportunities to receive and express sophisticated vocabulary and syntax.** Early childhood teachers, as a whole, regularly read aloud beautifully written picture books and informational texts throughout the year for many reasons, one of which is to support children's language development. We want children to hear well-crafted text and increasingly more sophisticated language patterns and vocabulary. It makes sense, then, for children to muck about in these types of books and try on the sophisticated language patterns and specialized vocabulary as they approximate reading these texts themselves.

- **Rich picture books and informational texts give children more meaning to negotiate and more opportunities for using a variety of comprehension strategies.** When beginning readers have a reading diet consisting of early level texts exclusively, they are mostly word-driven readers, and the name of the game is decoding, which is certainly part of the process of learning to read. Although early level texts are vital for learning strategies for decoding words, they may offer limited opportunities to engage with the text and think deeply about it. Children race through these books, despite all of our instruction and encouragement to slow down, linger, and grow ideas about them.

Of course, there is meaning-making work in any text, including Level A texts with one or two words on the page, and we teach children to have thoughts about what they're reading, whether it's a book with one word per page or a thousand words per chapter. That said, the early level books have tightly patterned text, rather thin and quick story lines, if there is one at all, and if they're early level informational texts, they can provide only very simplified information because the words are controlled to match the decoding strategy work children do at these early levels.

It's important to complement the important reading work children are doing with early level texts with the different kind of reading work they can do with rich picture books and informational texts, which we've described throughout this book.

BEGINNING THE YEAR IN KINDERGARTEN AND FIRST GRADE

Most kindergarten and first-grade teachers begin the year with children who are quite diverse as readers, both in their abilities and their attitudes toward reading. Children who've had very limited experiences with books before they begin school find themselves reading alongside children already decoding words with ease and confidence. It's important, then, to begin the year with a tone of invitation and inclusion around reading and let all children know they have reading powers, whether or not they're reading the words.

There are several ways teachers can use familiar, unfamiliar, and informational texts to help children see themselves as capable readers right from the start.

Launching Reading Workshop in Kindergarten

In Chapter 9 we described the start of a kindergarten year, where children shop for books from tabletop book bins filled with a variety of texts, including familiar and unfamiliar picture books, informational texts, ABC books, concept books, and so on. The books in these bins will change over the first month or two as read-aloud texts are added as well as smaller versions of shared reading texts. Teachers show children how they can read these books, and the children then "shop" for them to read during independent reading time. As children read, teachers confer with them in much the same way they'll soon confer about leveled texts—meeting children where they are and teaching something that will help them move along as readers.

At the end of this chapter, we've included possible teaching points a kindergarten teacher might consider for minilessons, conferences, or small-group instruction while launching reading workshop.

Emergent Story Book Reading

In Chapter 2 we described the work of Elizabeth Sulzby (1985) that showed the power of reading aloud picture books repeatedly over the course of a week or so. Once children have heard the book four or five times, multiple copies become available for children to read independently. Their familiarity with the language and events of the stories helps them make their way through the texts on their own.

From day one, kindergarten teachers can begin reading aloud these emergent storybooks, helping children become quickly and deeply familiar with many texts. This is especially supportive of English language learners and children who've had limited exposure to books prior to kindergarten. Launching reading workshop and committing to regular emergent storybook reading right from the start help children quickly self-identify as readers and expose them to a wide range of texts.

Moving Through the Year in Kindergarten

Although it's hard to predict exactly when it will happen, at some point many children in kindergarten will be ready to read conventionally. We'll know they're ready when we see them:

- recognizing some to many letters
- recognizing some to many letter–sound relationships
- recognizing some easy sight words (i.e., *the, my, I, mom,* etc.)
- understanding that letters go together to make words stay consistent (i.e., the word *mom* isn't *mom* on one day and *monkey* on another day)
- writing some words with beginning letters and some ending letters
- attending to the words in a text or recognizing that the text holds meaning
- exhibiting early reading behaviors (i.e., book handling and orientation)
- showing enthusiasm for learning to read
- beginning to read some environmental print (children's names, signs, etc.)

When more than half the children are ready for conventional reading, the teacher shows them how to find their just-right books, which are usually leveled texts. Children shop for just-right books they can read conventionally using strategies, and instructional time during reading workshop is now focused on strategies to decode, read with fluency, and make meaning. During independent reading, children are expected to practice strategies in books that are just right for them.

At this point, children should still shop for books that interest them but that they may not be able to read yet conventionally, though these books won't be the focus of reading workshop. Teachers might give children time to read and explore these books during partner reading, or they might add an extra ten minutes to workshop or find time at another part of the day. Books children choose to read are still an important part of their reading diet.

FIRST GRADE

By the time they begin first grade, most children read conventionally at a range of proficiency levels and continue to need instruction to become stronger at reading with accuracy, fluency, and comprehension in their just-right books. That said, most teachers spend a couple of weeks at the beginning of the school year teaching children expectations for reading workshop, inviting them into the world of first-grade reading, and building a community of readers. Children are likely to find all kinds books in tabletop book bins, both leveled and not, in a variety of genres, topics, and types. The teacher spends time these first couple of weeks assessing readers, determining their strengths and struggles, and figuring out each child's just-right reading level.

Once teachers have determined reading levels, children in first grade are expected to shop exclusively for just-right books so they can sharpen their reading skills and use a variety of strategies on texts that match them as readers. This makes a lot of sense when we're working on improving readers' skills, but there's more to reading than achieving a target accuracy rate or moving up levels.

First-grade readers are six- and seven-year-old children who have interests, passions, and curiosities that may not be found in their just-right books. For example, consider Franki, a first-grader who loved to bake and cook with her grandma, who watched *Cake Boss* and other cooking shows on TV, and who dreamed of being a "fancy baker" someday. There weren't really any books at her reading level—D—that had anything to do with her passion for baking. Sometimes she brought in cookbooks or magazines to read during her free time. She didn't read them conventionally, but she read them avidly. She studied the fancy cupcakes, and she would look at the ingredients lists for words she recognized like *butter*. She asked classmates to pick out their favorite cupcakes, and she put sticky notes with kids' names on those pages. The level D books didn't make Franki want to read. The cookbooks and magazines and photographs of fancy cupcakes did.

In every classroom there are children just like Franki whose interests aren't nurtured in books with dots on them, children who lug video game books, toy catalogs, and superhero comic books to school hoping for a chance to look at them or show them to a friend. We applaud first-grade teachers who carve out time each day for children to read whatever they want to read. Children should feel secure that every day in school, they'll have a chance to be the boss of their reading. They'll get to choose the text and do the work they want to do in that text.

Some might worry that providing the chance to read the "exciting" texts might create confusion or disappointment for children when they have to read their just-right books. We haven't found this to be the case, especially when a teacher:

1. sets clear expectations that during reading workshop, children read self-selected, just-right books to become stronger readers who'll be able, eventually, to read anything they want to read

2. builds at least ten minutes of read anything time into the daily schedule so children trust that this read anything time is as valued and consistent as any other important daily schedule items

3. supports children during read anything time with conferences, little reading tips, and enthusiasm for what they are reading

Providing time for children to read anything they want is important for all readers, but it may work special magic for reluctant readers or for children who find reading a challenge. These children benefit from choosing and engaging with books they love on topics that interest them. For example, we've worked in classrooms with reluctant readers who whine about reading leveled texts, but who can hardly wait to get their hands on the new informational book about dogs or the newest picture book by Mo Willems. We've seen children who get fidgety after five minutes of just-right reading time, but who could easily spend triple that time engaged in books about knights, football, or horses. Oftentimes, these books can lead reluctant children toward reading more than their leveled books can.

We want to be clear that we are not suggesting teachers squeeze in ten to fifteen minutes of read anything time with a busywork sensibility. When children are reading anything, it's important for teachers to have conversations and conferences with them. There are many things we can teach them as they explore any text, in addition to what we teach them in their just-right texts.

Possible Teaching Points Across a Year

As we think about reading instruction across a year, we consider possible teaching points we can make during daily read-aloud times, shared reading times, or within minilessons. Of course, anything we teach to the whole class can also be taught to children during individual conferences and small-group instruction. The following charts provide a starter set of teaching points focused on supporting children's meaning making, reading language, and independence before they are reading conventionally or in texts far beyond their proficiency level.

The charts do not include everything we think young children need to be supported as readers and writers. Providing instruction and opportunities for young children to learn and use other literacy skills, such as letter and word study, knowledge of letter–sound relationships, phonemic awareness, phonics, early sight word acquisition, independent writing time, and writing workshop, are all critical for children to become strong readers and writers. These components of instruction are outside the boundaries of this book, however, as our purpose here is to suggest ways we can support children's reading identities, meaning-making skills, and independence with texts. We consider this to be vital instruction *in addition* to teaching decoding skills, not *instead of* teaching them.

The teaching points are not broken out by grade level, although we considered doing that. As we created charts for pre-K, K, and 1, we realized there was quite a bit of overlap. Also, we always try to keep in mind we're teaching young children, not grade levels. After all, it's not uncommon for a preschool teacher to work with a child who is a proficient decoder, while a first-grade teacher confers with a child whose reading is more characteristic of a preschooler.

Rather than conferring with the child's age or grade level front and center, we look at what the child is doing with texts and decide how to support what comes next for him as a reader, thinker, talker, and learner. We should note, however, that even though children in preschool, kindergarten, or first grade might need the same teaching points, the instruction often looks and sounds quite different depending on whether we're teaching a four-year-old or a seven-year-old.

Here's an example of what we mean. Say that as a parent one of the things you'd like your child to learn is to express gratitude to other people. When your four-year-old receives a birthday present from your neighbor, you might say, "Say thank you to Mrs. Ryder." If she's seven, you might just give her a nudge and a look to remind her to say thank you. When she's twelve she says a quick "Thank you" without prompting, but when you get home you say, "Be sure to write a thank-you note to Mrs. Ryder."

The teaching point in each case is the same—we express gratitude for other people's kindness, but the language used and the expectations for the expression of gratitude are differentiated and appropriate for the individual child's development and experience. The grade level is not the starting point when we're figuring out what to teach. The child's work is the starting point, and although a teaching point might work for a range of grades and ages, we would adjust our language and approach depending on the child's age and previous experiences.

When supporting children to read books they're unable to read conventionally, a preschool teacher might offer the same teaching point as a first-grade teacher, but the frame for the teaching would be different. Figures 10.2 and 10.3 show how one teaching point can work for three very different learners, in terms of age and grade.

Teaching Point: Readers Can Study the Pictures to Read What the Character Is Feeling

Possible Preschool Version Reading Conference	Possible Kindergarten Version Reading Conference	Possible First-Grade Version Reading Conference
Teacher: "Look at the the little girl's face. How do you think she's feeling?" Child: "Sad." Teacher: "The little girl is sad. Why do you think so?" Child: (points to character's face) Teacher: "Oh, she's frowning? Her frown makes her look sad, doesn't it? Can you make that face? I'll try too. (they make frown faces at each other) You think she's sad because she's frowning. Will you read it telling how she feels?" Child: "She's frowning and sad."	Teacher: "When you're reading, you can look at the character's face to think about how the character is feeling, and you can say that." Child: "She looks sad." Teacher: "Why do you think so?" Child: "Her mouth looks sad and her eyes look sad, too." Teacher: "Will you say it like you're reading it?" Child: "The little girl is sad. She has a sad mouth and sad eyes because she lost her bunny."	Teacher: "One of the things you can do is to look for clues or evidence in the picture to help you figure out what the character might be feeling. A way to do that is to look closely at the character's face and say what the character might be feeling." Child: "She is really sad and frustrated." Teacher: "Sad and frustrated? What are your clues about that?" Child: "Well, she looks sad, like she's going to cry, and she left her bunny in the machine but her dad doesn't know it. He doesn't understand her so she's frustrated." Teacher: "Will you read it like that?" Child: "Trixie is sad and frustrated. She's going to cry because she left her bunny in the machine, but her dad doesn't know it, and he doesn't understand what she's trying to tell him."

Figure 10.2

Teaching Point: Readers Can Read Information Books by Using Exact Words and Teaching Language

Possible Preschool Version Reading Conference	Possible Kindergarten Version Reading Conference	Possible First-Grade Version Reading Conference
Child: (points around the page) "Bugs bugs bugs …" Teacher: "There are a lot of bugs on this page. Do you know what they're called?" Child: "A fly?" Teacher: "Yes, that's a fly. This one is an ant. What about this one?" Child: (shrugs shoulders) Teacher: "Hmm. Is it a wasp or a bee?" Child: "A bee, I think." Teacher: "Me, too. So we see a fly, a beetle, and a bee (points at each one) … anything else?" Child: (shakes head) Teacher: "OK, will you read it using the exact words? Instead of saying 'bugs bugs bugs,' you know exactly what they're called—a fly, a beetle, and a bee. Will you read it like that?" Child: "There's a fly, a beetle, and a bee …"	Child: "Oh, look at the bugs." Teacher: "When you're reading informational books you can use the exact words, you know. Like here, instead of saying 'That's a bug' you can say, 'That's a fly crawling on a wall.' Will you try this one?" Child: "A bee?" Teacher: "Yes…, that's a bee." Child: "Flying in the flowers." Teacher: "Read it like that." Child: "That's a bee flying in the flowers." Teacher: "Keep going." Child: "That's an ant walking on the sidewalk."	Child: "Bugs can be everywhere, on the walls and on the ground and in the flowers and stuff." Teacher: "One of the things you can do when you're reading informational books is to sound like an expert by using expert words—using the most exact words you can. Instead of just saying 'bugs,' you can be more exact, more of an expert. Do you know the more expert word for bugs?" Child: "Insects." Teacher: "Yeah. Now instead of 'Bugs are everywhere,' it would be 'Insects are found everywhere.' Keep going using exact expert words." Child: "Flies are in houses flying around and climbing on walls, and ants crawl for long ways on sidewalks. Bees buzz around flowers to get food."

Figure 10.3

As you can see, the same teaching point works across grades because all three children need similar nudging, but the teaching sounds different to accommodate the individual child. With that understanding in mind, here are some possible teaching points to support children when they read books they can't yet decode.

Early-in-the-Year Teaching Possibilities: Establishing and Strengthening Reading Identities

Our priorities:
We are a community of readers.
We can read books even if we can't read the words.
We can share books with each other.
We can find books we want to read.

READERS TAKE CARE OF EACH OTHER AND THEY TAKE CARE OF THEIR BOOKS.

What can we do to take care of each other and to take care of our books?

- We can carefully turn the pages and put our books back so they're not on the floor.
- We can use bookmarks to reserve our place for the next time.
- We can invite others to read with us.
- We can ask each other about what kinds of books they like to read.
- We can appreciate all our differences as readers because the differences make us a very strong community.

READERS CAN FIND BOOKS THEY WANT TO READ.

What do we do as readers, and how do we find books we want to read?

- We can find books we want to read by looking at the covers and saying, "This looks interesting . . ."
- We can find books we want to read by looking for books someone has read to us already.
- We can find books we want to explore because no one has read them to us yet.
- We can find books that match our interests.
- We can read books our friends love.
- We can find books that have characters we know.
- We can look through a book once to see how it works and then read it again.
- We can find interesting stuff in books.
- We can choose the same book over and over and become experts at reading it.

READERS HAVE LOTS OF WAYS TO READ.

What do we do when we can't read the words?

- We can read the pictures by looking at them closely and telling what we see (making meaning).

- We can read the pictures and describe what is going on (determining importance, summarizing).

- We can read the pictures and say what the characters are doing (noticing and naming).

- We can read the pictures and figure out what is happening (inferring, predicting, making meaning).

- We can read the pictures and think about why things are happening (inferring, interpreting, activating schema).

- We can read the pictures and think about why characters look like they do and do the things they do (inferring, connecting, activating schema).

- We can remember how the book goes and say what we remember (recalling, retelling, activating schema).

- We can remember whatever we can about what's in the book (recalling, retelling, activating schema).

- We can look closely at characters' faces and talk about how they are feeling (inferring).

- We can say more than one or two words for a page (elaborating).

- We can connect one page to the next by using words like *and then*, *after that*, and so on.

- We can say as much as we can for each page by studying what is in the picture (elaborating, using text evidence).

- We can read informational books and make it sound like we're teaching something (genre distinction, determining importance).

READERS CAN SHARE BOOKS WITH EACH OTHER.

How do we share books with each other?

- We can find a friend to read with.

- We can find a book that our friend might like and invite our friend to read with us.

- We can read the book together by looking closely at the pictures.

- We can pick the same book over and over and become experts at reading it with a friend.

- We can read the book by saying as much as we can about the pictures.
- We can act out characters or parts of the book.
- We can recommend a book to someone who might like it.

Please also see the conferring charts in Chapters 3, 5, 6, 7 for other teaching ideas.

Mid/Late-in-the-Year Teaching Possibilities: Meaning-Making Strategies and Building Independence and Oral Language

Our priorities:
We can make meaning in any book.
We can read books independently and help ourselves if things get tricky.
We can use all we know about how books go so that we can
read storybooks or informational texts.
We continue to offer support and reinforcement of any early-
in-the-year instruction that children may still need.

READERS HAVE WAYS TO UNDERSTAND THEIR BOOKS.

What can we do to make meaning in any book?

- We can imagine what the characters might be saying or thinking.
- We can use specific sounds effects we remember from the book, or we can make up sounds if it's an unfamiliar book.
- We can keep reading if we have a question about a book to see if we can find an answer.
- We can talk about books with friends to help us understand them better.
- We can look at the words to see if we know any of them and to see if they can help us understand.

- We can use language that matches the kind of book (i.e., storybook language/ informational text language).
- We can use what we know from our own lives to help us understand what's going on in a book.
- We can figure out what seems to be the most important part of the picture/ illustration and read that.
- We can tell the story of characters across pages.
- We can connect one page to the next to tell the whole story.

READERS CAN DO THINGS TO HELP THEMSELVES IF READING GETS TRICKY.

What can we do to read independently and to help ourselves if things get tricky?

- We can do any of the above to help ourselves read books.
- We can look through the book at least once to get a sense of how it goes and then reread each page.
- We can go back and reread if we get stuck.
- We can think about what we remember from the story if we've heard it before.
- We can make our best guesses about what's going in if we're not sure.
- We can make our best guesses if we think about what would make sense.

READERS CAN READ STORYBOOKS LIKE STORYTELLERS.

What can we do to read storybooks the best we can?

- We can make up dialogue as we read.
- We can pretend we're a character and read it like the character would.
- We can read the book by paying attention to the characters' expressions and saying the characters' feelings.
- We can read the pictures by saying where the characters are and where the action is taking place.
- We can read the beginning in a way that sounds like a beginning, and we can read the ending in a way that sounds like an ending, using what we know about storybooks.
- We can act out parts of stories by ourselves or with our friends.
- We can use all of the clues on the page (pictures, words we might know, etc.) to read the story.

- We can pay attention to what happens in the story and tell what caused it.
- We can use words we know in the story to read it in the best way.
- We can make the pages go together so it sounds like a real story.

READERS CAN READ INFORMATIONAL TEXTS LIKE EXPERTS.

What can we do to read informational books the best we can?

- We can figure out what topic the book/the page/the section is about and study the pictures.
- We can study the pictures and say, "I notice . . . and it makes me think . . ."
- We can think about what we already know about the topic to help us.
- We can read in a way that sounds like an informational text by using exact words (i.e., *ants*, not *bugs*) and teaching language ("The tongue is important for a frog 'cause it helps it get food").

Please also see the conferring charts in Chapters 3, 5, 6, 7 for other teaching ideas.

As these possibilities show, young children can be supported in so many ways as readers. These charts don't include everything worth teaching, but they're a good start, and our hope is that teachers will expand upon them as they observe their own students' idiosyncratic strengths and needs as readers. After all, when children choose what they really want to read, they are able to find themselves in the wonderful, diverse, and comforting world of books.

CHAPTER 11

Making the Move from Thinking About It to Acting on It

Many people make resolutions as the new year approaches, whether it's January first or the educators' new year, which comes in late August. Around those auspicious times, we say:

> "I'm going to get in shape this year!"
>
> "I vow to take better conferring notes."
>
> "This year, I'm going to do more volunteer work."
>
> "I'm going to sing every day with my class this year."
>
> "This is the year that I'm finally going to take that oil painting class at the museum!"
>
> "I'm going to be so much more organized!"

These sorts of resolutions feel so good to make. They're optimistic and sunny and full of hope. Unfortunately, all of the good intentions of our resolutions can fade away because having goals and resolutions isn't enough to make them come true.

It's one thing to say, "I'm going to run a marathon in this coming year!" and it's another thing to actually do it. It's one thing to say, "I'm going to take better conferring notes this year," but it's another thing to do so consistently. The missing link that gets us from having a goal to reaching the goal is an action plan.

A marathon? Hmm. When will you train? You don't like running during winter mornings, so will you find a running group to keep you going? To be ready for a marathon in the spring, what kinds of distance running do you have to do, starting now?

Better conferring notes? Hmm. What kind of system will you use? What kinds of information will you record? How will you make sure you see as many children as possible? How will you use your conferring notes?

Without a plan of action, sometimes our biggest hopes and most desired life goals fall by the wayside. We don't ever sign up for the spring marathon. This can certainly be true with respect to our teaching goals, too. We attend workshops or read professional texts about taking conferring notes, and we say to ourselves, "*Yes*, I'm going to do that!" or "This sounds wonderful." But we end up using our default conferring note-taking system, which is haphazard at best. If we don't have a plan of action, both our most inspired and noble intentions as well as our smaller or more modest goals can be difficult to realize.

We share this idea because we know how hard it can be to alter our teaching practice when the reality of the school year encroaches on our opportunities to fantasize about how we want it to go.

Once the school year launches, or when we're striving to keep on top of things in the middle of the year, it can be hard to redirect our children and ourselves to take risks as we try new approaches to teaching and learning. Although it's our sincere hope that the ideas and suggestions we shared in this text will inspire teachers to imagine new and different ways of viewing and supporting their children as readers before they're reading conventionally and when they're reading self-chosen, interesting texts they can't yet read conventionally, we also know that sometimes the having of new ideas isn't enough—we need an action plan.

Creating a Plan of Action

Just as each runner needs her own, differentiated action plan to reach her marathon goal, the same holds true of action plans for our teaching. They need to be differentiated for teacher personalities, school climates, and more. If a first-grade team wants to get better at keeping conferring notes, some teachers might want to figure out how to do this on an iPad, whereas other teachers prefer to write notes by hand. Perhaps they can agree on the content of the notes, but the format is likely to vary.

So as we consider an action plan to help teachers integrate the ideas from this book into classroom practice, we realize that there is no master plan or guide to implementation that we can offer. Instead, we have some questions that might help you make your own plan as you set goals for yourself and your children (Figures 11.1 and 11.2).

From Idea to Action: Preschool Considerations

Guiding Questions for Action Plans	Considerations
How many of the read-alouds each week will focus on supporting children in reading books they can't yet decode? One? Two? More?	In other words, during your read-aloud times, how often will you explicitly model strategies children can use when they read their own books (e.g., read-aloud time after lunch on Mondays/Wednesdays)?
What instructional topics will you address during read-alouds to support your children's independence and language growth as they read books before they read conventionally?	It's helpful to have a plan for what you might teach to support language and independence and then make adjustments as you observe children doing this work themselves (e.g., month 1: finding books we want to read; month 2: studying pictures and illustrations to figure out what's going on; etc.).
When will children have opportunities to read books themselves? What components in your day and spaces in your classroom will support this?	Having consistent and dependable opportunities for children to read by themselves can be included during center time, choice time, and other times. There might be library nooks, reading cushions, special chairs, and corners for kids to do their best reading.
When and how often will you observe children and support their reading through conferences?	It's important to organize for this effort by using class lists to be sure you're getting to all of the kids within a week and using a note-taking sheet of some sort to record what you observe.
How will you share student growth and change with caregivers? How will you involve caregivers so that they support this work at home?	Will you videotape children interacting with texts to show families the possibilities?

Figure 11.1

The answers to these questions will vary because of the wide range of preschool programs. Children in a full-day, five-day-a-week program would get more reading conferences and opportunities for instruction than students in a half-day program, for example. That's why it's so important for teachers to imagine how this work can fit into the special characteristics of their teaching situation.

From Idea to Action: Kindergarten and First-Grade Classrooms

Guiding Questions for Action Plans	Considerations
How many of the read-alouds each week will focus on supporting children in reading books they can't yet decode? One? Two? More?	In other words, during your read-aloud times, how often will you explicitly model strategies children can use when they read their own books (e.g., read-aloud time after lunch on Mondays/Wednesdays)?
What instructional topics will you address during read-alouds to support your children's independence and language growth as they read books before they read conventionally or when they choose books they can't read conventionally?	It's helpful to have a plan for what you might teach to support language and independence and then make adjustments as you observe children doing this work themselves (e.g., month 1: figuring out what's going on; month 2: studying pictures and illustrations to grow our ideas about a book; etc.).
When will children have opportunities to read familiar and unfamiliar picture books and informational texts, in addition to the time they need to read just-right books? What schedule components in your day and spaces in your classroom will support this?	Having consistent and dependable opportunities for children to read these texts is important. Ten minutes for free-range reading can be added on to reading workshop, can be tucked into the day, or can be a fine way to end the school day.
When and how often will you observe children and support their reading of texts they may not yet read conventionally through reading conferences?	Similar to the way teachers confer with children reading just-right texts, it's important to organize for this effort of supporting children when they read anything by using class lists to be sure you're getting to all of the kids within a reasonable time frame and taking notes of some sort to record what you observe.
How will you share student growth and change with caregivers? How will you involve caregivers so that they support this work at home?	Will you videotape children interacting with texts to show families possibilities and growth? Will you include information about this on progress reports?

Figure 11.2

e wish you lots of luck and collegial support as you give this work a try. Based on our experiences as we've worked with young children, we know that there will be many rewards, for you and for them, when they are supported as readers before they can even read the words.

Note-Taking Sheets for Conferences

Conferring Note-Taking Sheet

Student Name _____

Book Title _____ Date _____

Familiar _____   Unfamiliar _____   Informational _____

Language Level Observed _____ Independence Level Observed _____

Notes: (Strengths, Teaching Point, Next Steps, etc.)

Book Title _____ Date _____

Familiar _____   Unfamiliar _____   Informational _____

Language Level Observed _____ Independence Level Observed _____

Notes: (Strengths, Teaching Point, Next Steps, etc.)

Book Title _____ Date _____

Familiar _____   Unfamiliar _____   Informational _____

Language Level Observed _____ Independence Level Observed _____

Notes: (Strengths, Teaching Point, Next Steps, etc.)

Note-Taking Sheets for Conferences (Continued)

Conferring Note-Taking Sheet

Name: Title: Fam ___ Unfam ___ Info ___ Lang Level ___ Ind Level ___ Notes:	Name: Title: Fam ___ Unfam ___ Info ___ Lang Level ___ Ind Level ___ Notes:	Name: Title: Fam ___ Unfam ___ Info ___ Lang Level ___ Ind Level ___ Notes:	Name: Title: Fam ___ Unfam ___ Info ___ Lang Level ___ Ind Level ___ Notes:
Name: Title: Fam ___ Unfam ___ Info ___ Lang Level ___ Ind Level ___ Notes:	Name: Title: Fam ___ Unfam ___ Info ___ Lang Level ___ Ind Level ___ Notes:	Name: Title: Fam ___ Unfam ___ Info ___ Lang Level ___ Ind Level ___ Notes:	Name: Title: Fam ___ Unfam ___ Info ___ Lang Level ___ Ind Level ___ Notes:
Name: Title: Fam ___ Unfam ___ Info ___ Lang Level ___ Ind Level ___ Notes:	Name: Title: Fam ___ Unfam ___ Info ___ Lang Level ___ Ind Level ___ Notes:	Name: Title: Fam ___ Unfam ___ Info ___ Lang Level ___ Ind Level ___ Notes:	Name: Title: Fam ___ Unfam ___ Info ___ Lang Level ___ Ind Level ___ Notes:
Name: Title: Fam ___ Unfam ___ Info ___ Lang Level ___ Ind Level ___ Notes:	Name: Title: Fam ___ Unfam ___ Info ___ Lang Level ___ Ind Level ___ Notes:	Name: Title: Fam ___ Unfam ___ Info ___ Lang Level ___ Ind Level ___ Notes:	Name: Title: Fam ___ Unfam ___ Info ___ Lang Level ___ Ind Level ___ Notes:
Name: Title: Fam ___ Unfam ___ Info ___ Lang Level ___ Ind Level ___ Notes:	Name: Title: Fam ___ Unfam ___ Info ___ Lang Level ___ Ind Level ___ Notes:	Name: Title: Fam ___ Unfam ___ Info ___ Lang Level ___ Ind Level ___ Notes:	Name: Title: Fam ___ Unfam ___ Info ___ Lang Level ___ Ind Level ___ Notes:

Library Considerations

A Well-Rounded, Inviting K–First-Grade Classroom Library Might Contain . . .

☐ **Baskets of books representing various genres**
(i.e., picture books, narrative texts, list books, informational texts, poetry, biographies, wordless picture books, graphic novels, concept books such as alphabet books, counting books, shapes, colors, opposites, etc.)

☐ **Baskets of books gathered around topics**
(i.e., sharks, dinosaurs, Halloween, books about school, baby siblings, superheroes, flowers, etc.)

☐ **Baskets of books featuring individual authors**
(i.e., Ezra Jack Keats, Mem Fox, Donald Crews, Cynthia Rylant, Arnold Lobel, Mo Willems, etc.)

☐ **Baskets of books arranged by series**
(i.e., Horrible Harry, Frog and Toad, Poppleton, Piggie and Elephant, Pigeon, Cam Jansen, etc.)

☐ **Baskets of books that support the work of the current unit of study or inquiry**
(i.e., during a poetry study: poetry by Arnold Adoff, poems about nature, silly poems, shape poems, etc.

☐ **Leveled book baskets that represent the range of learners and their projected growth**
(i.e., depends on your particular leveling system and the text needs of your students

☐ **Baskets that contain texts other than books**
(i.e., Sunday comics, maps, cards, Internet material, etc.)

☐ **Baskets that contain "kids' picks"**
(i.e., books we love from home, favorite books from kindergarten, top ten funniest stories, etc.)

☐ **Shared reading texts and multiple copies**
(i.e., Mrs. Wishy-Washy, Hungry Giant, poems from shared reading time, etc.)

☐ **A basket containing texts the teacher has read aloud**
(i.e., multiple copies of these texts, etc.)

☐ **Baskets containing readers' tools**
(i.e., sticky notes, bookmarks, graphic organizers, if necessary)

Other Classroom Library Considerations:

Location: Where is the library in the classroom?
Changes: How does it change to reflect the work, time of year, and so on?
Design: Is it visually appealing and organized so that young readers can find books?
Access: How do students borrow and return books?
Responsibility: Are there whole-class expectations for taking care of books?

Key Descriptors Tip Sheet

Key Descriptors for Familiar Book Language Levels (FLL)

FLL 1	FLL 2	FLL 3	FLL 4
• Attends to illustrations • Names and labels objects and actions • May not connect one page to the next • May not rely upon recall of the story	• Uses more detail when naming objects and actions • May connect one page to the next occasionally • Relies on schema to read with more content accuracy	• Expresses familiarity • Connects one page to the next to form more cohesive text • Reads with more content and language accuracy that's true to the text	• Expresses familiarity and uses schema to read • reads with high level of accuracy—content, language, and syntax • Reads with expression and intonation that matches tone of text

Key Descriptors for Unfamiliar Book Language Levels (ULL)

ULL 1	ULL 2	ULL 3
• Attends to illustrations • Names and labels objects, and actions • May not connect one page to the next	• Uses more detail when naming objects and actions • Uses words to connect one page to the next (**and then, then**, etc.) • May infer characters' feelings • May infer events that aren't represented in illustrations	• Elaborates more for each page; sounds like sentences instead of phrases • Uses sense of text and literary language to connect pages • Imagines dialogue • May editorialize about text or illustrations

Language and Independence Level Grids (Continued)

Unfamiliar Book Language Levels (ILL) and Independence Levels (IL)

ULL 3
- Elaborates more for each page: sounds like sentences instead of phrases
- Uses sense of text and literary language to connect pages
- Imagines dialogue
- May editorialize about text or illustrations

ULL 2
- Uses more detail when naming objects and actions
- Uses words to connect one page to the next (*and then, then,* etc.)
- May infer characters' feelings
- May infer events that aren't represented in illustrations

ULL 1
- Attends to illustrations
- Names and labels objects, and actions
- May not connect one page to the next

IL 1
- May resist or say, "I can't read"
- Frequently appeals to an adult for help
- May need a prompt or nudge for each page
- Relies on an adult for help to start to read and to continue reading

IL 2
- May say, "I can't read" at first
- May need a prompt or nudge to get started but quickly takes over after a page or two
- May talk to an adult about text but rarely to appeal for help
- Relies mostly on pictures, text schema, or content knowledge to move through text

IL 3
- Self-initiates reading
- Reads with or without an adult
- Resourcefully uses pictures, schema for text, and/or content knowledge to read independently
- May ask an adult a question about content but quickly moves on independently

Language and Independence Level Grids (Continued)

Informational Book Language Levels (ILL) and Independence Levels (IL)

IL 3
- Acknowledges that text teaches about a topic
- Uses domain-specific vocabulary
- May include own schema for topic (accurate or not)
- Relies upon prior experiences with informational text to sound like an informational text that's teaching something

IL 2
- Elaborates more when naming items, objects, and actions
- Uses words to connect one page to the next (*and then, then,* etc.)
- May switch between reading the text and editorializing about the topic or pictures
- Sounds like a story more than an informational text

IL 1
- Attends to illustrations
- Names and labels objects, and actions
- May not connect the pages
- Reading may not reveal any schema for how informational text might go or sound

IL 1
- May resist or say, "I can't read"
- Frequently appeals to an adult for help
- May need a prompt or nudge for each page
- Relies on an adult for help to start to read and to continue reading

IL 2
- May say, "I can't read" at first
- May need a prompt or nudge to get started, but quickly takes over after a page or two
- May talk to an adult about text but rarely to appeal for help
- Relies mostly on pictures, text schema, or content knowledge to move through text

IL 3
- Self-initiates reading
- Reads with or without an adult
- Resourcefully uses pictures, schema for text, and/or content knowledge to read independently
- May ask an adult a question about content but quickly moves on independently

WORKS CITED

Allington, Richard, and Rachael Gabriel. 2012. "Every Child, Every Day." *Educational Leadership*, 69: (6) 10–15.

Allington, Richard, and Anne McGill-Frazen. 2012. *Summer Reading: Closing the Rich/Poor Literacy Gap*. New York: Teachers College Press.

Calkins, Lucy. 1994. *The Art of Teaching Writing*. Portsmouth, NH: Heinemann.

Calkins, Lucy, and colleagues. 2014. *Units of Study for Teaching Writing: A Curriculum*. Portsmouth, NH: Heinemann.

Christ, T. and X.C. Wang. 2010. Bridging the Vocabulary Gap: What Research Tells Us About Vocabulary Instruction in Early Childhood. *Young Children*, 84–91. Accessed at http://www .naeyc.org/files/yc/file/201007/ChristWangOnline.pdf.

Clay, Marie. 2005. *Literacy Lessons: Designed for Individuals, Part One*. Portsmouth, NH: Heinemann.

Collins, Kathy. 2004. *Growing Readers*. Portland, ME: Stenhouse.

Dewey, John. 1887. *My Pedagogic Creed*. University of Chicago.

Duke, N. K. 2000. "3.6 Minutes per Day: The Scarcity of Informational Texts in First Grade." *Reading Research Quarterly* 35: 202–24.

———. 2003. "Reading to Learn from the Very Beginning. Information Books in Early Childhood." http://journal.naeyc.org/btj/200303/InformationBooks.pdf.

———. 2004. "The Case for Informational Texts." *Educational Leadership,* 61 (6).

Duke, N. K., V. Purcell-Gates, L. A. Hall, and C. Tower. 2006/2007. "Authentic Literacy Activities for Developing Comprehension and Writing." *The Reading Teacher,* 60: 344–55.

Dweck, Carol. 2007. *Mindset*. New York: Ballantine Books.

Federal Trade Commission. 2012. "Ads Touting 'Your Baby Can Read' Were Deceptive, FTC Complaint Alleges." http://www.ftc.gov/news-events/press-releases/2012/08/ads-touting-your -baby-can-read-were-deceptive-ftc-complaint.

Glover, Matt. 2009. *Engaging Young Writers*. Portsmouth, NH: Heinemann.

Johnston, Peter. 2004. *Choice Words: How Our Language Affects Children's Learning*. Portland, ME: Stenhouse.

Leung, C. 2008. "Preschoolers' Acquisition of Scientific Vocabulary Through Repeated Read-Aloud Events, Retellings, and Hands-on Science Activities." *Reading Psychology* 29 (2): 165–93. ERIC Document Reproduction Service No. EJ790593.

New York City Department of Education. 2003. "Prekindergarten Performance Standards." http:// schools.nycenet.edu/offices/teachlearn/PreKStandards.pdf.

Ray, Katie, and Matt Glover. 2008. *Already Ready.* Portsmouth, NH: Heinemann.

Robinson, Kenneth. 2009. http://www.theguardian.com/education/.

Sulzby, Elizabeth. 1985. "Children Emergent Reading of Favorite Storybooks: A Developmental Study." Reading Research Quarterly, 20:458–481.

Teaching Channel. 2014. "How They Do It in Sweden." https://www.teachingchannel.org/videos/examining-pre-school-curriculum.